BURNING THE PAST

BURNING THE PAST

Essays on Change by the Students of
John Marshall Alternative School

8 2 6
SEATTLE

Book printing by Westcan Printing Group, Winnipeg, Canada.
CD printing by Polar Bear Productions, Winnipeg, Canada

ISBN 0-9779832-1-8

826 Seattle
8414 Greenwood Avenue North
P.O. Box 30764
Seattle, Washington 98113
(206) 725-2625
www.826seattle.org

826 Seattle is dedicated to helping young people improve their expository and creative writing skills through free tutoring, mentoring, workshops, and other writing programs.

TABLE OF CONTENTS

Foreword

Let's think about change. What distinguishes change from the same old? One thing: When you are in a situation of the same, you are in a situation of repetition—meaning, you want the future to be the same as the present and the past. When you are in a situation of change, you are in a situation of invention. To change anything means to be creative in the face of an open future. It is to this reason alone (a situation of creativity) that change owes its difficulty. The same is always easy because it is known; to change is to deal with the unknown.

In these pieces by young writers from John Marshall Alternative School, the reader is confronted with two unknowns: one, the writer who you don't know and must discover; two, the writer's subject itself, change—what are they going to become, what will they discover in the open future? What will shock them into a new awareness? And so to read these works is to be as creative as the writers. In the end, it's not all about reality, it's all about creativity.

Nothing in the world is neat, and this volume is further proof of this fact. Though it's about change, it's also about many things. Why? Because many things come with change. (Only one thing can come from the same: the same.) With a fury that defines youth (an age of heated self-creation), these stories rush out in every direction and bring back to life, through the medium of words, many worlds with many possibilities, difficulties, hopes, beliefs, and desires. You will be impressed (indeed, overwhelmed) by what is here. These are not dead words, but words that are alive and expressing at every moment situations of intense self-discovery and self-creation—change.

Charles Mudede

Introduction

What do I possibly have to say about change that these students haven't said already? When I read their stories, I am amazed at their ability to adapt to the changes thrust upon them. I am in awe of their incredible resilience. Like most people I know, I have never experienced anything like the challenges these kids face, sometimes every day. Reading these pieces is an exercise in empathy.

Working with 826 Seattle on this project has been a teacher's dream. People often compliment educators on the work we do, commenting on how difficult it must be. Many parents and community members spend time volunteering in our schools. But, I have never seen a group of people like the volunteer writers, readers, and editors from 826 Seattle descend on a John Marshall classroom, determined to help the often intimidating students stick with a huge project. I have so much gratitude for these individuals. They share the belief of many that public school students rarely get the attention they deserve. They are also willing to donate their often scarce time to make sure that, for a few short weeks, each student has a chance to sit down with an adult to discuss his or her writing and the process for making it better.

When we decided that the theme for this year's book would be "change," John Marshall Alternative School was slated for closure at the end of the 2006-2007 school year. It has since been given one more year, maybe more. We exist year to year here, never knowing for sure if we will be open the next year, who the teachers will be, which students will return, who will be new. Out of twenty-three John Marshall students who wrote essays in last year's book, *It's Not Always Happily Ever After*, only three students came back to the school this year. Most of the forty-seven middle- and high-school students included in this year's book are new to Marshall. I suspect many of them will not return because, as you will read, frequent moves and changes in housing are the norm. In short, this is not a group of students who haven't already experienced major life changes.

People often romanticize their youths, perhaps forgetting how little control children have over their lives. I believe that being a child is excruciatingly difficult. Even if children have what can be classified as a "happy childhood," they are essentially powerless. Most of the big things—where they live and with whom, where they go to school, even sometimes how they dress or wear their hair—are decided by someone else.

I love this 826 Seattle project, because it gives all the young people who choose to participate a sense of control. Yes, we adults did pick the theme, but it's a broad one. The students decide exactly which part of their lives (or a fictional character's life) to write about. Students collaborate on the book's title, cover, and design, and they are even given the chance to veto the suggestions of their copyeditors. How often does that happen in the classroom?

One of my favorite moments this year was when several students asked me why anyone would want to read the writing of a bunch of Marshall students. I told them about the 300-plus people who came to the publication party last year. I told them about the libraries in Seattle, California, and Colorado that ordered copies, and how a class of teacher-candidates in the Seattle area was assigned the book as required reading. I told them that last year's book sold all over the United States. I told them it sure seemed to me that people were interested in their stories and that I could guess why: the stories of their lives are interesting, thought-provoking, and full of lessons for everyone.

So, what does this ultimately mean for the student-writers themselves? Will their lives somehow improve now that they are published authors? I think so. I know that students have come out of this project with a much better understanding of the process of writing, which makes them more likely to continue with their own writing. If the results of last year's project are any indication, they will also enjoy a fantastic evening at the publication party, where friends, family, school staff, and community members will gather to celebrate their accomplishments. The students will autograph these beautiful books, and one or two may ask their adoring mother to assist by opening the book to the autograph page (as a student did last year). Maybe those who move on to another school district will present the book with pride to their new teachers, asking the teacher to look through it to see if he or she recognizes any of the authors (as another student did). Or, perhaps they will use their experience as the springboard for an illustrious writing career.

And how about the readers? What would I like them to take from these stories? Obviously, the students have their own intentions for readers, and I dare not try to speak for them. As their teacher, I simply want parents, community members, and other readers who care about children to try to see things through their eyes. Remember what it was like to be twelve, fifteen, seventeen. Ask yourself how you can help a child grow into an adult with grace and dignity. Remind yourself how much children depend on us to guide them, and remember to do so as well as you possibly can.

Audra Gallegos
Teacher
John Marshall Alternative School

IT'S SO HARD FOR ME TO
THINK OF MYSELF AS A
MOM, BUT NOW I NEED
TO GROW UP.

Stuck in the Middle
Emma Lopez

Change is not always bad. Life is change. Life would stand still if there wasn't any change.

The most important changes you experience happen as you grow up. Your parents may treat you like the world is filled with roses and everything is beautiful and kind. My mom always hid everything terrible from my sister and me. She tried to raise us in a world that did not exist. She wanted to keep us away from harmful and dangerous things; she wanted us to be safe.

As I grew older and understood things more clearly I began to realize how the world really was. My dad was, and still is, an alcoholic, and there was never a day when I didn't see him drinking. There was no day when he was free of that. My mom told him to leave the house because we did not deserve to be under that influence.

At the time I was living in Mexico and I was happy there near my family and friends and in the lovely weather. I didn't expect my mom to decide to move. She never said anything about not liking where we lived, and she seemed happy to be around our family.

We had no choice about the move; my mom was determined to leave the country in search of a better life for us. When we arrived here in Seattle I was very excited; I was eight and thought we were just visiting. Boy, was I wrong. The days turned to weeks, then months, and finally years.

I was mad at my mom for bringing us here. I wanted my friends and family and the beautiful Mexican weather. What I loved most there was the huge powerful sun and the heat. You woke up with the rays of the sun shining on your face; every day was a pleasant day without rain or fog. And there were plenty of beautiful beaches you could go to for fun, not like here in Seattle, where the water is almost freezing.

I attended a bilingual program at the TOPS School for about a year to learn to speak English, then I was switched to Coe Elementary. Learning English was pretty easy. I remembered everything they taught me, but I was embarrassed to talk to people because I had an accent. That's why making friends in my new school was difficult for me. But after my first year in Seattle I got used to the weather and the fact that I had to speak English.

When I started middle school I wanted to change the way I dressed because my mom and my sister were asking me why I dressed like a boy and telling me I should wear skirts and dresses. I hated that so much; it's my life and I should have the right to do and wear whatever I want without anybody saying anything.

Thinking that way didn't get me anywhere though. Sometimes my mom would buy me clothes I didn't like. Skirts, tight shirts, jeans, or anything that looked too girly I would hate. I took that crap for about a year, and then in the summer between sixth and seventh grade I got my hair cut and straightened and bought new clothes. The first day of seventh grade people looked at me with shock. Had I really looked that bad before?

As the school year went on boys started to talk to me. I felt weird because I wasn't used to getting attention from boys. But by January I had started to go out with my boyfriend and we have now been together for more than a year.

My mom didn't have a problem with him at first, but then she started to say things that weren't true. She told me I should leave him because I was too young to have a boyfriend and also because he was a bad guy. She thought he smoked and drank like my dad, but she was wrong. My mom was always insulting him and judging him by the way he dressed, and that made me mad.

I never understood her rage against him because she could never just sit down with me and talk about her issues with him. She is not a calm person, and for some reason she likes to argue. She could see I was happy with him. That's what I didn't understand; I thought she wanted me to be happy. My boyfriend was getting tired of her insults, and that made him dislike her.

Now I was stuck in the middle. I had to listen to my mom's insults and also my boyfriend's. My mom said I always took his side when I should be agreeing with her, and he said it wasn't like I cared that he was insulting my mom. Of course I cared, and I tried explaining but he never listened. So I avoided conversations about my mom. But the story doesn't end there.

When my boyfriend and I had been going out for about nine months, we found out I was pregnant. Millions of thoughts went through my mind, and the first one was, How am I going to tell my mom? It was in September when I got pregnant and the first few months were not the best. I threw up every day, and I still had to go to school.

The only people who knew were my boyfriend, my sister, and me. When I was about thirteen weeks along my boyfriend and I told my mom, and she was furious. It seemed like her hair was going to burst into flames. I was scared she was going to hit me the minute my boyfriend left. She didn't speak to me for a few days, but she did take me to the doctor to get my prenatal care.

When we arrived at the hospital for the prenatal visit I felt like everyone around me knew that I was pregnant. It seemed like everyone was pointing fingers at me and whispering things with hatred on their faces, like it was a sin to be pregnant. As we walked to the check-in area I kept my head down and just stared at the floor. We waited for about five minutes but it felt like an eternity. When I heard my name, my hands started to sweat and when I stood up my legs wobbled. We made our way to the room and waited for the doctor.

I hated when there were moments of silence, because every time there was silence my mom said harsh things that made me cry. Ever since we told my mom I was pregnant, I couldn't keep in the tears. Finally the doctor came in and asked what was wrong, and my mom told him with anger and disappointment in her voice. Again the tears gushed out of my eyes. I was angry with myself; never before in my entire life had I cried the way I was crying now. I wiped my tears and listened to the questions the doctor was asking; then he handed me a little container for a urine sample.

He left to look at the results to see if I really was pregnant. When he came back I was hoping he would say I wasn't, but deep down I knew I was, remembering the pregnancy test I had taken three weeks earlier. I could see the fury and disappointment in my mom's eyes.

I went back to the hospital two weeks later because they had to go over my health history and take blood samples. That day I got to see my baby through a little ultrasound monitor. The doctor looked at the baby and took measurements to see how far along I was, then she let me see my baby. The instant I saw my baby I felt overjoyed and proud. I couldn't believe that a human being was growing inside of me. For the rest of the day I just couldn't stop thinking about my baby.

I can understand the anger my mom had about me being thirteen and pregnant, but now I need a lot of support, especially from her.

I don't regret getting pregnant, but I regret being young and pregnant. Being pregnant is one of the most important and best things that has happened to me. As my tummy gets bigger and the weeks pass, my pregnancy feels more real. It's so hard for me to think of myself as a mom, but now I need to grow up. I need to be strong for my baby and me. For now, I'm just waiting patiently for the time when I can finally hold and love my baby.

Fourteen-year-old **Emma Lopez** thinks
that this book project was a "good
way to get youth writing." Emma likes
reading and sleeping, and she plans
on finishing school and being a good
mother. What Emma likes most about
herself is her friendly, happy, and
caring personality.

SHAKEENA, YOU ARE A
BEAUTIFUL RED ROSE
THAT HAS BLOOMED
INTO THE CENTER OF MY
HEART AND SOUL.

SheShi's House of Angels
Rasheeda Davis

My mother, Keesha Jackson, knows the meaning of sacrifice. She cared for my ailing grandmother from the time she was a young girl until my grandmother's death in 1997. My mom always tells me stories about how she had to begin taking care of her mother at a very young age. While other children were out playing in the St. Louis neighborhood where my mother grew up, she was inside the house doing everything she could to help. When I ask my mom how she felt about having to stay in a lot, she says she still felt loved and the home was serene. "Just the two of us," she says.

Then when my mother was a teen she and her mother moved to Seattle, where my mother had her first child, my big sister, Shakeena. A few months after Shakeena was born my mom said that Shakeena's features started to change. When my mom took her to the hospital, doctors took lots of tests so that they could see what was wrong with her. When Shakeena's test results came back my mom found out that she had cerebral palsy, which is irreversible brain damage that causes an extreme curvature of the spine. This causes pressure on her heart and lungs and seriously impairs her ability to breathe. Soon it became clear that Shakeena would never be able to walk, talk, or take care of herself on her own.

Ena, as we called her, was born a week before my mother's eighteenth birthday. I always wonder how it was for my mother to raise Ena without having the other parent's help. After Shakeena was born my mother no longer had time to go to parties, because she would always be at the children's hospital. I give my mother lots of props because there are young teen mothers who would rather go to a party than sit in a hospital with their sick child. If my mother wanted to she could have chosen to give up, but she made the choice to take her responsibility even though the father didn't want to and he did exactly that, nothing to help my mother raise my sister.

Later my mother gave birth to my older brother, Mikal, the middle child, then William, and then me, Rasheeda, the youngest of four. The three of us at very young ages (I was only eight) noticed that our mother was carrying this very large burden alone so we managed to learn how to work Shakeena's feeding machines, because she had a tube in her stomach, which is how she took all of her nourishment. I have known how to work Shakeena's feeding tubes since I was five years old. As I got older I started doing her long thick hair and helped wash her laundry that always needed to be cleaned.

In 1999 Ena started getting sick again and the doctor told my mom that she might not live. Even though doctors had already given Shakeena six months to a year to live, we never thought about losing her. September of 1999 Shakeena went into a coma. My mom decided to give Shakeena a birthday party because she had a strong feeling that my sister was waiting for her fourteenth birthday, which wasn't until October 21. So the next day we had lots of friends and family over to celebrate Ena's early birthday.

Shakeena was still in a coma but my mom decorated her bedroom with balloons and streamers. Everyone was enjoying themselves and taking pictures with Ena for memories. When it was time to sing to Shakeena, my mom lit the candles on the cake, held the cake over Shakeena, turned off the lights, and everyone began to sing "Happy Birthday." As we were singing Shakeena started smiling and came out of her coma—everyone was so excited.

When her birthday party was over our cousin asked William and me if we wanted to stay the night at her house until the next day, because Mikal was going to his dad's house. Before we left I went upstairs to give Shakeena a kiss on her warm forehead and told her that I loved her and I would be back tomorrow, and told her "Happy Birthday" one more time. As I left Ena's room I saw my mom and told her that I loved her too.

The next day was Sunday, September 26, 1999, a day that I will never forget. It was 11:30 a.m. when our cousin came into the bedroom to tell William and me that we had to go home, because we had to get ready for school the next day. As we were getting dressed I noticed that my cousin India was crying, but I wasn't paying attention to what was going on. I just though that she was in trouble or something. When we all got in the car William, my cousin Kamari, and I were sitting in the back seat laughing at each other like we always do; we are all very close in age. But my big cousin Angela and her two teenage daughters were very quiet as my cousin India sat in the back with us younger kids and my cousin Rashonda sat in the passenger seat while Angela drove us home. When we were about halfway home Angela turned down the music and that's when my whole world came crashing down. While she was driving she said to William and me, "I am not going to lie to you guys. Ena passed away this morning at 11:00 a.m." All I remember was everyone in the car crying—and my cousin India reached her arms out and hugged me until I got home to my mom.

When we finally made it home I walked through the door and went straight into the living room where my mom was on the phone crying. When my mom saw me crying and I saw her crying she immediately got off the phone and tightly wrapped her arms around me. I did the same and she said, "It's okay," but I knew really everything was not okay. When I stopped crying for a second I asked my mom where Ena was, and she said upstairs. So I quickly went upstairs where I saw Shakeena lying in her bed. I guess it was true what my mom said: Shakeena was waiting for her birthday party, and deep in my heart I knew she enjoyed it.

I love Ena, and I have this message for her: "I will never let your place in my heart be taken and you will never be forgotten. Shakeena, you are a beautiful red rose that has bloomed into the center of my heart and soul. Bye, big sister, but not forever."

It was about two weeks after my sister Shakeena's death and we still had people from out of town giving our household the kind of support we all could use. But it still didn't feel as if I had lost my big sister, which left me being the only girl. Most of the time when I felt like crying I would go to my mom and cry like a big baby, and she would rub my back and say to me, "Everything is okay. Ena is in a better place, and she is not suffering anymore, she's with Grandma."

When people ask me about my sister they always ask if I remember her, as if I was too young to understand. I let them know that she was a big part of my everyday life. I would see Ena from the time I woke up to the time I went to sleep. Shakeena and I shared the same room and lots of special memories. One of the things I will always remember is when Shakeena would bat her eyes two times when my mom would tell her to say SheShi, which is my nickname, and Shakeena would always laugh. I always think about the big smile that she would have on her beautiful face when she would hear Mr. Rogers from the TV show Mister Rogers' Neighborhood sing; that was her favorite show.

The day after Ena's funeral an old friend of my grandmother's named Tommy came over with her friend Patrica, and Cora, Patrica's daughter. Cora also had cerebral palsy. So as Patrica let down the wheelchair ramp so that Cora could get out of the van, my mom started to cry as soon as she saw Cora, because she resembled Ena. They both had the same kind of hair and a lot of the same features. It was weird that Cora had on the same color dress my big sister was buried in. I think that's what touched my mom the most.

My mom told Patrica that she was certified to work with disabled kids, because Patrica was looking for someone who could help her out with Cora. Patrica had one amputation and she could really use the extra help. Patrica told my mom that she would soon have another amputation so she wanted my mom to start when she was feeling better. When my mom told me that she would soon be working for Patrica and Cora I was proud of her, because that was a huge step after losing Shakeena, working with another child with cerebral palsy and not knowing what the outcome could be.

Five months later my mom was working with Cora, going to her home every morning at 5:45 a.m. to get her ready for school, then waiting for her school bus to come. When Cora was off to school my mom would take the time to clean the whole house, when her job was to just make sure Cora's space was clear. When it was time for Cora to come home after school my mom would already be there to get her off the bus and she was always on time. My mom would stay at Cora's until it was time for Cora to get a bath and go to sleep. When my mom would come home after work she would make sure that my brothers and I were ready for the next day.

A few months had passed and it was time for Patrica, Cora's mom, to have surgery so that meant that Cora would be staying at our house until her mother was healed from surgery. When Patrica went into surgery she was expecting to have her foot amputated but when she came out of surgery her leg was amputated. Doctors said that it was better to just amputate her leg because infection had spread. So that meant Patrica had to go into a nursing home to heal and Cora would be staying with us for a few more weeks. Weeks turned into months and Patrica was still in the nursing home and Cora was still being taken care of by my mom. When it was time for Patrica to get out of the nursing home she would be needing lots of help for herself and Cora, so my mother told Patrica that she could move in until she was all better.

So there it was; Cora and her mother Patrica were living with us in our four-bedroom house. Cora and I shared a room, Mikal and William shared a room, Patrica had her own room, and my mom had her own room. It was a total of fifteen months that Cora lived with us and a total of five months her mother lived with us, and all I could see in the back of my mind were memories of my mother taking care of my grandma, and my sister Shakeena, all over again. It was a pleasure for her to be able to care for Patrica and Cora, being able to help a mother and daughter with the experience that she learned from taking care of her own mother and daughter. Mom, I think you are a very inspirational women and you will always be blessed in whatever journey you decide to take next.

Out of everything my mom, my brothers, and I have been through, those experiences only made us stronger and changed the way we think and the way we treat others because you never know what could happen to that person, but at least you know when that person's gone you did everything you could do.

Since Shakeena's been gone, every day is a struggle for our family but we refuse to give up; we just think about the positive and how we were able to give other families advice and information for their disabled children. My brothers and I know how to do things that many older people would be confused by even if they tried. I just thank Allah every day for giving my family the chance to share our story in newspapers and pictures in calendars encouraging families going through the same thing—don't give up!

Rasheeda Kiara Davis would like to thank 826 Seattle and John Marshall Alternative School "for this opportunity to pour my heart into this book." Now fifteen, she says she feels blessed by her wonderful family and hopes to build one of her own someday—but not before becoming a pediatric nurse. Until then you can find her braiding hair, hanging out with friends and family, and "living life to the fullest."

I FOUND OUT IT WAS
EASIER TO STAY OUT OF
TROUBLE. LIKE MY DAD
SAYS, "IT'S EASY TO GET
IN TROUBLE, BUT HELL
TO GET OUT."

I Grew Up a Screw Up
C.J. Thomas

Ever since I can remember I was always in trouble. A terror since the grade school era. Bathroom passes, cutting classes, squeezing girls' asses. It got to the point where every day I went to the vice principal's office. He got so sick of me he put my name on the chair and said, "When you come in, sit here and put your head down. I don't want to see your face." I got kicked out of class on purpose. I didn't like this one kid in my class, this big guy I hated who was a bully. He made my two years there hell doing things like hitting me in the gut as hard as he could so my chest would cave in and I couldn't breathe. The school wasn't all bad though, just him.

In the second grade I transferred to Stevens School. It was a new, better school but by fourth grade I got kicked out for fighting. A kid called me names, but then it got worse, because he shouted a racist comment about my dad. So I chased him down the hall, caught him by his shirt, and hit him in the back of the head. He rolled over and tried to get up, but I didn't give him time. I got on top of him and let him have it. When he got up, his face was bloody and his shirt was ripped.

So I got kicked out. I really liked Stevens. I had been there for three years, all my friends and some family went there, even my best friend from preschool. The other kid just got suspended.

I went to a new school called Laurelhurst. I felt out of place. It was ninety-six percent white, one percent Asian, one percent black, and two percent other. I didn't mind that; Stevens was similar. But at Laurelhurst they looked down on me for being black. One day I was on the computer and the class bully walked up and tried to kick me off. I held my ground. Since we had a sub that day, the bully felt invincible. He started to call me names and push me, saying stuff like, "Hit me, I dare you!" So I did.

I have big hands, so I made his lip and nose bleed. After that he was hysterical, screaming stuff like, "Oh my god, you broke my nose! Help me, help me!" He wasn't a bully anymore. Blood was everywhere—on his clothes, the chairs, the floor, even on the sub.

The next day, my regular teacher said, "It's obvious you know how to fight better than him. But next time let me or a staff member handle it. That way there will be less blood. I hate blood." Luckily for me, I knew her from when she was my teacher in preschool.

That same day it happened again, but this time a security guard came and got in the way and he accidentally caught a couple of hits too. He called the police. They came and handcuffed me and shackled my legs to try to scare me. They told me I was going to jail and I was expelled from school. But I didn't care. I didn't like that school anyway.

They took me to the station and I sat in the holding tank for three hours until my mom came and got me after work. It wasn't the first time I'd had a run-in with police.

One time in third grade I cut school and got picked up by the police. But the funny thing was I lied and talked the policewoman into giving me a ride to the house along with my friend Shan. I told her we went to a private school and had a half day and were going to my house. I had her drop me off a couple houses down so she didn't see where I really lived. We went to the park and stayed until she drove away.

Anyway, by this time my mom and dad were really worried. I haven't lived with my dad since I was four, but he is still in my life, sometimes more than I like. My mom said someone called CPS (Child Protective Services) and I might get taken from her. I thought she was trying to scare me, but the next day a man from CPS was at my door. I was in the other room watching TV. I didn't care. I thought my family wouldn't let CPS take me, but if they did I would go live with another family. I was young and dumb. My mom and her boyfriend (who ironically was a cop) were talking in the living room with the person from CPS. My mom was really worried that she might lose her only kid. He didn't take me, but he kept tabs by calling my mom until school started in the fall. I started a new school, an alterative school for grades K-8 called Wilson Pacific. I was in fifth grade. It was nice. I liked it. I was in a small class with kids I knew from other schools. It was fun. But I hated my teacher. So did my home girl Shantial. So one day we walked out of class and went to my house, which was about three blocks from the school. We came back with silly string, water balloons, and toilet paper, and let his class-room have it. We got suspended for the rest of the year, but it was only about a week.

I came back the next year and the teacher was gone. Things got better. Since it was an alternative school, I didn't get suspended as much. Plus it was my last year in elementary school, so I was just enjoying it. But I wound up fighting a teacher. He called the principal so I went to her office. She was nice; I liked her, so I didn't mind going to Barbara Saylo's office.

While I was in the office talking to her, the teacher called the police. Before I knew it I was surrounded by the principal, a cop, the teacher, and another teacher who had witnessed the fight. I knew the cop from other run-ins. He tried to arrest me and I wasn't having it, so I tried to fight him. He slammed me to the ground super hard, but

I went down swinging. He won, but I got in some good hits. He held me in cuffs so tight that after he took them off, my wrists showed the indent of the cuffs for hours.

My mom came to the school. Since I was only ten, juvie wouldn't take me. The cop told my mom I was going to a group home. Mom said, "It was only a matter of time before you got took." She cried. All I could do was sit there.

The group home was a nice one in Queen Anne called Seattle Children's Home. This place really helped me. I think it was because I saw lots of older kids, some almost eighteen, who had messed up their whole lives. No education, doing any drug they could get their hands on, all screwed up in the head. That's when I realized I had to change and try to do my best in school and do something with my life. I stayed at the Children's Home for about eight months. It was cool. We did stuff like rock climbing, and we could earn money so I wasn't broke.

When I got out, it was summer. I decided that I would go into the military when I got older. I went to a summer camp, and I loved it. The friends you make at camp last forever.

One of the counselors was a football coach, and he recruited me for Lake City Junior Football. My mom was scared I would get hurt, but she said it was a great way to "channel my high spirit." I took to it like a fish to water. I am still friends with the team and see them around town. I have played every year since, except one.

I went back to the alternative school the next year for sixth grade. After a couple of months the school closed and all the middle school students went to John Marshall, an alternative school for grades 6–12. It was different, lots of gangs and fights. I was called out on my first day. So I fought. My mom and dad were disappointed yet again, but my dad really helped me. He said, "All the strength, spirit, heart, and energy you put into fighting—channel it into football." So I did.

I love high school football, but it's very different. We practice more and work harder. The bonds, the new friends, the parties, the fans, the pranks we pull on each other and new guys and, most of all, the cheerleaders! I still see the guys from Lake City Junior Football. We play each other for high school now. It's fun to play against them.

John Marshall Alternative School was different from what I was used to. My friend Mike and I were the youngest ones in the program, and we decided to prank the school. In science we read about how if you drop a feather and a penny they fall at the same speed. So Mike and I decided to try it, only we used whatever we could get our hands on: books, pencils, pens... even a chair. We dropped things from the third floor to the first in the main stairwell. I was at the top and Mike was at the bottom, and I would drop stuff when he told me it was all clear.

The principal at Marshall has a loud voice, and Mike heard the principal as he turned the corner, but he had already told me to drop the book I was holding. Mike ducked into the restroom, which was about five yards away. The book almost hit the principal in the head. After that Mike and I had the respect of the middle-schoolers, and the upperclassmen looked at us like little brothers. Unfortunately, we did get caught, but we didn't care. Earning everyone's respect made it worthwhile.

As I got older, I got in more trouble for fighting teachers. In sixth grade I got arrested for assault and went to juvie, but the charges were dropped. Same thing in seventh grade, but that time I got probation. In eighth grade I got charged with felony assault. I did diversion (probation and community service and whatever else the judge wanted) and the felony never touched my record.

I really changed in ninth grade. I was on probation for the felony, so I was super good. I found out it was easier to stay out of trouble. Like my dad says, "It's easy to get in trouble, but hell to get out." I think I also grew up. I realized it was time to get good grades and plan for adulthood.

Two people really helped me a lot: Heidi Schuler and Art Kono.

I think if it wasn't for Heidi I would still be in trouble, in and out of juvie, a ward of the state, who knows? I owe a lot to her! I didn't have her as a teacher until I was in high school. But I saw her around the halls and went to her class for various reasons. She had a lot of the big homies in her class. She helped all of them graduate and do something with their lives. She was always nice to me. Once I got in her class she pushed me to be the best I can be. Not to do the minimum work, but to do my best and the maximum. She held me to a higher standard than any other teacher, a higher standard than I set for myself, for that matter. Even now when I'm in the halls and she sees me she yells at me to go to class, even if it is during break. She says to be in class early. She does it to everyone. I think it's because she cares so much, too much, if you ask me. The worst thing is, she is in touch with my mom so now I can't slip. My mom has a great ability to look very disappointed in me that always results in me feeling bad.

The other person who helped me is Art Kono. He always has my back, fighting for me no matter what. He's the house administrator for our school, and I've always looked up to him. He doesn't take any crap from anybody. Whenever I get mad he says the same thing, "Be cool, you can't accomplish anything when you're mad." Even now, when I get frustrated in the process of transferring schools, he says, "Be cool. I got this. You just do your thing. And keep the grades up and the behavior good." I owe him a lot too.

I'm now in tenth grade and in the process of transferring to Ingraham High School, where I have a starting spot as center on the varsity football team. GO RAMS! Mike is a junior at Chief Sealth so I don't see him anymore. I have a job. My mom and dad couldn't be prouder. I plan on going to college on a football scholarship, then the NFL. If that doesn't work out, I want to go into the military. I get in trouble every now and then. Nothing too serious. I haven't been arrested since eighth grade and don't plan on it. The police still harass me and my friends because of our pasts. Pull us over, search us, and question us. But what minority don't the police harass? I see a lot of my homies dead or in and out of jail, the pen, and juvie. And I know I don't want to be another black statistic!

"My parents both grew up poor, but they still did something with their lives," says sixteen-year-old **C.J. Thomas**, and for that reason they are his inspiration. C.J. loves sports, as well as fishing and playing video games. What did C.J. think of the book project? "It's nice to be able to say, 'I am a published author!'"

WHEN MY REPORT CARD
CAME, I WAS SO
NERVOUS, BUT FOR THE
FIRST TIME IN MY LIFE I
HAD FOUR A'S AND TWO
B'S. I WAS SO HAPPY I
CRIED. I PUSHED MYSELF
AND BROKE OUT OF MY
GLASS BUBBLE AND
SMELLED THE FRESH
AIR OF CHANGE.

Change of Heart
Ashley Mackay

The change in my life started like any day would, but it ended how no one would want it to. I was eleven years old and next door at the neighbors' apartment with my mom when we heard a knock at the door. As the door swung open my dad stood there, wearing nothing but his pants.

He said, "I shot myself. I'm bleeding."

"It's a joke," I thought at first, then, "Oh my god." He'd shot himself up through the jaw. Blood was squirting out and pouring all over his chest and the floor.

My mom rushed Dad to our apartment next door. I was in shock. I walked out the front door and followed a drip trail of blood down the front step, around the corner, and inside.

Mom yelled, "Go check what happened upstairs." The rail and steps were stained with my father's blood. I wandered into their bedroom and saw the gun on the bed, and what looked like some practice shots fired into the wall. I followed the trail back out and around the corner to the bathroom. Blood was everywhere. I went back downstairs and my mom and her friend had towels, wiping Dad's chest and plugging his throat.

Outside, the neighbors looked frightened, curious, and worried, saying things all at once: "I heard gun shots." "What happened?" "Are you all right?"

I was in a daze. All I could focus on was the dark sky with flashing lights and the sound of sirens in the distance rushing to our aid. My stepgrandmother Adella ran up and embraced me. "Are you okay?" she asked.

I finally let it in and broke down in tears as my grandfather Dean grabbed me and held me tight, patting me on the head and saying, "It'll be all right. It's not your fault."

Tears streamed down my face as I watched the cops inspect our home while the paramedics in the kitchen got my dad ready for the ambulance. He'd used our friend Troy's gun (which was in my closet) to shoot himself, and the bullet was three-quarters of an inch from his brain, applying pressure. Shards of metal were lodged in his sinuses.

Questions filled my head and wouldn't stop: Why? What made him do it?

Adella drove me to the small hospital, but they'd airlifted him immediately to Salt Lake City. The doctors in Elko weren't experienced enough to handle the problem. She took me to her house and I walked in and sat down in my favorite chair, but soon went to bed without saying anything.

In the following days, my mom told the mother of an ex-friend of mine that my dad shot himself. The mother told her daughter. Because this girl hated me, she told the entire school what happened. The kids at this middle school were religious and cruel. They'd always disliked me, but now I was the freak of the school. They pushed me into walls, down the stairs, and spread rumors that my family was cursed. They called me a voodoo witch, a druggie. Not only did they make fun of my family, they started in on everything about me personally, from my natural features to what I wore. I became deeply depressed.

I went to a therapist who said I should be more like the people at my school, to fit in so they wouldn't judge me. It seemed he was trying to turn me into the kind of person I despised the most and put words in my mouth that weren't there. I told him over and over that the girls at my school were slutty, anorexic, and mean. I became suicidal and tried to kill myself several times; when my therapist found out he tried to put me into a mental hospital. I felt I was better off dead, so why not make it happen? I hated the world, I hated myself, and I hated everyone but my cats. My love for them kept me from going a little deeper, pulling a little tighter, or taking a larger amount of pills.

My father has had depression all his life. My mother's constant abuse and drug use didn't make it any easier. At the time my dad shot himself, his best friend Troy was staying with us to save money to get his own apartment. After all this happened, my mother divorced my father. When he got out of the hospital, his mother took him back to Washington to stay with her to recover, both physically and mentally.

Soon my mom and Troy started dating, then moved in together. We moved into a double-wide trailer on the outskirts of Elko. When my mom and Troy decided to get married, it was a shock to me and to his kids. At the time we met them, Annie was nine and the twins, Sylvia and Alex, were seven. I wouldn't have been able to survive all of my problems without my stepsiblings—they are the joy of my life. The first time I visited them in Vegas, I loved it. I felt in the right place. My usual fear of people dissolved. They came and visited us sometimes in Elko.

I stayed in touch with my dad, talking to him on the phone and sending him stuff. He wanted to come visit but didn't know when. One day when Troy's kids and I were in our pool, I saw my dad walking up. I stopped and gasped, then jumped out of the pool and yelled, "Dad!" I leaped on him and hugged him hard. We got to talk and visit until we succeeded in getting closer.

To top off everything that was happening and changing, my mom started doing drugs again. She had been doing drugs all my life, on and off, but more on than off. I hated it. She sat in her room all day smoking drugs or she left for hours. I was in a terrible state. I craved my mom's attention but she told me I wasn't important enough to receive it. Deep down I'd always hated my mom but at the same time I loved her and wished everything bad would go away so we could be a regular mother and daughter. I was stuck in this fantasy for a long time and I wished every day it would come true.

When my mom wasn't on drugs she was a good mom, but that life was never good enough or fulfilling for her. She wanted the party life. Not only did I hate how she and the others acted on drugs but also I hated what they did, to each other and to me.

One day when I was six, I walked into the family room and my mom and aunt were sitting there. A big wooden box sat in the family room—not a crate but a box with no gaps or holes. My mom grabbed me and shoved me into the box and closed the lid and hatch so I couldn't push it open. It was dark and I was cramped.

I screamed at the top of my lungs. "Let me out, let me out!" I tried to kick and bang on the sides, and I started to cry and hyperventilate. I begged her to let me out, over and over. I was running out of air; I got dizzy. "I can't breathe, let me out!" I tried again, but they still didn't. I could hear them laughing.

I lay there sobbing for ten minutes or so, and suddenly the lid opened. I got up and fell out of the box.

They laughed and said, "Oh, you'll be all right. You should've heard yourself. You were so scared."

I crawled across the floor until I could stand, then staggered off crying. Since then I've been claustrophobic and have a hard time trusting people.

With everything going on in my life, I decided school was too hard and put a hold on it. We moved again, this time into the sagebrush in an outlying town called Spring Creek. I spent most of my time on the Internet. I came up with the idea to look up the problems I had on the web and learn more to help myself. To get over my fear of people, I would try to venture from my family in stores and talk to people on my own.

Mom and Troy decided to have my brother Timothy. I'd never had much practice with babies and I was afraid I would drop him. I had my own problems, anyway. I didn't want to deal with a baby.

My dad tried to find a job in Elko but wasn't successful and stayed with us off and on as a roommate. Troy's job was going downhill and we began to think of somewhere new to move. I mentioned I would like to move back to Seattle and Troy's kids agreed they thought that would be a good idea, since the twins were born there. After two months, it was decided. I was upset about having to leave my grandparents but I needed to get away and start off new.

When we arrived we stayed in a motel. A job that had been promised didn't happen. We searched for months and months trying to find work for Troy, still living in motels. My mother started on drugs again and found connections. It became worse than it had been for a long time; she'd leave and be gone for hours, which turned into days then weeks at a time. She'd take the van so we couldn't go anywhere unless we took the bus. When she was around, she brought her drug buddies over, or just came home to shower and change, or steal something to trade for drugs. Troy finally got a job, but by then she'd given up taking care of Timothy. Now it was up to me although I was only fifteen.

The first day I was left alone with him was horrible. I had never changed a diaper, fed a baby, or anything. I was stepping into the dark with no clue except for what I'd watched Troy do. I'm a fast learner so it only took a few weeks to catch onto Timothy's routines: when his naps were and when he got hungry.

It was really hard to take care of him when I was fighting with my mom all the time, fighting because she'd bring all these people into our small motel room, up to ten sometimes. I'd fight with her to make them leave but I wasn't strong enough. I'd been submissive all my life. I'd always let people walk all over me.

Back in Spring Creek I'd started cutting myself to deal with my depression but had stopped. Now my heart was so full of anger, sadness, and hatred that I couldn't bear to keep it inside anymore and I started cutting again. Time after time I fought with her and time after time I couldn't stand up enough to her to force them out. They'd wake up

Timothy, or she'd trade what little food we had and our food stamps for drugs or money.

One day I opened the door while I cleaned our room. It was pouring rain outside and I love the sound and smell of rain. One of Mom's drug buddies came by and said my mom would be by in a minute. I agreed to let him inside, thinking I wouldn't have to be alone for long. He sat in the chair while I straightened up and asked me personal questions, and why I was so nervous. He kept asking why I wouldn't date him and I kept telling him because I had a boyfriend. I didn't, but I was fifteen and he was twenty-one.

I sat on the edge of the bed and he said, "There's something on your hip."

I got up and turned to look and he slapped me on the butt. I whipped around and moved to hold the door open and said, "Please leave immediately."

He said, "Hold on, no need to get worked up."

"Please leave. I asked you nicely."

After he walked out, I closed the door and locked it and shut the curtains. I sat on the bed, then curled up in a ball and cried. It's always been hard for me to feel close to any male, and this made it worse. It took me two years to be able to hug and tell Troy I loved him.

After about a half hour I heard a knock on the door. It was my mom and the guy. She wanted in and I said "No, not with him." She started ranting at me, saying she'd break the window if I didn't let her in. I screamed back at her but she wouldn't stop kicking the door, so I finally opened it. Even after I told her what he did, she didn't care. It hurt me deep inside, but that was the beginning of my change.

Things got worse and worse. One day Mom brought home another guy and they went in the back room. My mom kept coming out, turning up the volume on the TV. When I went back there to say something she covered him up quickly. They pretended they weren't doing anything, but they were.

I went to the bathroom filled with anger, sadness, and hatred. I wondered how she could do that to Troy after everything he'd done for her. I wanted to go back there with the butcher knife I kept by the door and kill them both, but I stopped myself and cut slice after slice on my arm instead, until there were ten or so cuts and blood streamed down my arm into a puddle on the floor.

I walk out of the bathroom and the man handed me twenty dollars and left. I shoved my bloody arm at my mom and yelled, "I hate you! Look what you made me do." I was crying uncontrollably.

All she said was, "Can I borrow that twenty?" She took it out of my hand and left. I was heartbroken, but I stood up for myself after that.

Day after day, week after week, month after month, we struggled with no van when she was gone. Troy and I took the bus everywhere or walked to find organizations to help us pay for rent, or food banks. I got bruises where grocery bags cut into my hands from carrying so many for so long, walking or riding the bus. After moving from motel to motel to temporary housing, we moved in with my dad. By this time my mom was in one of her "off-again" periods when it came to drugs, but she still had the DTs.

Living with my dad was actually quite refreshing, but at night I would lie awake and thoughts about the past would race through my mind. I had horrid nightmares and woke up panting and in a puddle of sweat. I dreamt of all the horrible things I had gone through and woke up crying and fell asleep the same way.

I'd started seeing a therapist in temporary housing and continued when we moved to Dad's place. After going there on the bus every week and dealing with people, I started to become calmer and look forward to it.

We got kicked out of Dad's place and finally moved to an apartment. After two weeks Mom was back on drugs worse then ever. I got a lock for my bedroom door so she couldn't take anything of mine, but she figured out how to break into my room. She blackmailed me saying if I didn't give her money terrible things would happen to her, or to us. I fell for it every time because I didn't want to take the chance that she was telling the truth. After a long excruciating fight, I would give in.

It was getting closer to the beginning of the school year. I knew that I needed to go back and get an education and make up the two and half years I'd lost. I had become a little more comfortable out in the world, but that wasn't enough. I needed to talk to people and get used to other teens. When Troy's church offered to let me come to their camp for a week, I hesitated. I didn't want to leave Timothy alone for my mom to take care of, and I was worried about my room. I knew camp was what I needed though, so I agreed to go and packed my stuff.

The first day we went hiking. I sucked in my breath and squeezed my phobias and pride tight; I went up to everyone and introduced myself. To my surprise everyone in the group was nice and willing to be my friend and included me in things. I've always loved archery and my first time trying it was there. I was a natural at it and won first place in an all-camp competition. I opened up one of the last days I was there and told the group a little about myself. I explained how much I appreciated how nice they were to me even though I didn't follow their religion. I had a wonderful time at camp; it was like my whole soul was rejuvenated and new.

When I got home it was a complete disaster. I could barely see the floor for all the stuff all over it, and my mother went back to bed after letting me in, without saying a word. I went to my room and discovered that my game system and four hundred dollars worth of video games were missing. After getting into a fight over it, she left again. I managed to track down the game system and one game, but the others were gone forever.

School started shortly after that and I was so nervous. I held my breath, though, and chatted with people when they were talking about things I was interested in or knew about. Going back to school was hard at first, especially with putting up with my mom at the same time and babysitting Timothy. But I really wanted to catch up, so nothing got in my way or slowed me down.

I soon made a few friends, and I surprisingly caught up quickly in school after missing so much time. I put my nose to the book and worked ahead in the classes when teachers would let me. I didn't talk or daydream. I asked for help and made friends with the teachers. When my report card came, I was so nervous, but for the first time in my life I had four As and two Bs. I was so happy I cried. I pushed myself and broke out of my glass bubble and smelled the fresh air of change.

Although I was changing, my mother wasn't—at least not for the better. She kept getting worse. Our fights got worse, both verbally and physically. The thing I hated the most and drove me to violence was when she would bring drugs home and do them in the bathroom or the bedroom when Timothy was asleep, breathing in the smoke. That disturbed me so much I picked fights to get her to leave. I would take everything that was bottled up inside of me out on her; I wanted her to suffer and feel what I felt. I was having anxiety attacks all of the time. With my asthma, it was frightening.

Now guys were coming to our door all the time harassing us for money Mom owed them and demanding to know where she was. Our door was kicked in. When she came home I would scream at her, "You don't love me, you don't care. Leave and don't come back. Nobody wants you!" One time I lunged and we fell into the closet and broke the door. I hit her and choked her and screamed, "I hate you!" It took both Troy and my dad to pull me off of her and still I was lunging, trying to jump back on her. Even after that she walked out the door and said she'd be back later, like none of it had happened. I broke down crying, I fell to the floor shaking and sobbing until I had an asthma attack. My body was so limp, sore, and heavy that all I could do was lay motionless in a puddle of drool on the floor. I couldn't speak because my throat hurt so badly from screaming and crying. Anxiety attacks this bad happened at least once a month.

The rage within me built up more and more, and even after exploding on my mom or carving my body up, it still didn't relieve the pressure in my heart. I began to think of suicide again and tried quite a few times. I hated life. School was my only escape from home, and I looked forward to being there every day. To cope with the problems at home, I became a workaholic and did massive amounts of homework so I had something to zone out on and forget for a while.

It took Troy a long time to realize Mom wasn't going to change. I knew life with her was just a roller coaster: everything's good when she goes up but everything eventually goes bad again when she goes down. Troy was more vulnerable to her threats of prostitution, and gave in more easily than I did.

The teachers at school noticed the cuts on my arms and were concerned for me. I wanted to tell them everything but I was afraid of Child Protective Services (CPS,) because I knew if they got involved, Timothy and I would be taken away. Foster homes aren't as peachy as they make them out to be—I know, I've been in my share. I didn't care what happened to my mom, I cared about my brother. The day she decided drugs were more important than taking care of her newborn son was the day I became his new mom.

Not only did it change my perspective on not liking kids, it helped form my personality and maturity. I have always been there for him and as far as I'm concerned, I'll be the only mom he'll ever need. Troy did his fair share when he wasn't at work or dealing with my mom, but I've done everything a mother is supposed to do. I've taught Timothy most of what he knows. I discipline him and I've taught him to express love with hugs and kisses. I didn't have to, I chose to, and I don't regret it. He's my brother, my son, and the joy of my life.

On our days off, Troy and I would try to get out as much as we could to get away from her. We'd take Timothy to the park or we would go to the beach or the mall. After the bad start we had at the beginning, Troy and I formed a close bond. One of my favorite things to do for my anxiety and depression was to spend a summer afternoon at Shilshole Park and then sit on the beach as day turned to night, watching the bonfires, listening to the distant music. I just laid back and watched the sea and sky, letting all of the bad feelings in my heart fade away, letting happiness replace it for the time we were there.

We got evicted from the apartment, but we found the place we are in now and we've been here ever since. It only took Mom a few days in the new place to find not only one connection but four. After a few weeks, a bounty hunter came to the door and claimed her for jail. We had just found out she was pregnant. Because she was so skinny and malnourished from drugs, the baby was, too. While she was in jail Mom claimed she'd found religion. She'd changed and was a new person and everything was to be forgiven and would be different.

Mom was in jail for about a month or so and those were the happiest weeks I'd seen in a long time. Troy and I did family things all the time. We gathered back all the things we lost with her gone and started to have a home instead of just a roof over our heads. When she came home, she was sober and well behaved. Like all good times with her, it lasted a couple months before going bad again.

When my mom gave birth, my baby sister Emma almost died during delivery. Because Emma had a skin disease, she had to stay longer at the hospital under a special light. Troy and I suspected that Mom might have cheated on Troy and now we were pretty positive. Emma had darker skin than anyone in Mom's or Troy's families, and she had bluish brown eyes and dark brown hair. At first we were in denial, saying that it was just from the skin problem. I would say how her eyes looked green even though I knew they were definitely brown.

Emma and Mom both tested positive for drugs when Emma was born, so naturally the hospital told CPS and we were investigated. For about a month or two, my mom had to get random drug tests every week and go to outpatient rehab meetings. We were interviewed by our caseworker and evaluated. Troy and I worked tooth and nail to keep the kids at home. The very day after we got everything settled and Mom didn't have to take drugs tests any more, she disappeared and went back on drugs again. I had known Mom would end up abandoning Emma, too. Sure enough, she left the entire responsibility to me, and I love Emma as much as I love Timothy.

Troy's kids were coming for a family reunion over the fourth of July and we were so excited to see them. The first night was exciting, seeing each other again and them seeing Emma for the first time. We went to Sequim on the fourth of July as a remembrance to Troy's sister, who'd died that day the year before.

The last day Troy's kids were with us, we planned on getting up early to go to the zoo, but instead I woke to Troy and Mom fighting. It was a bad fight, and Troy called the cops. My mom was arrested and the cops came and got a police report from everyone. Soon after, we left for the bus and went to the zoo without her. We had fun and spent a few hours there, then went to see the second Pirates of the Caribbean movie, which was really cool.

That summer was the best I'd ever had. We got rid of all her stuff, rearranged the apartment, and got set on a routine. We did something fun just about every day; we went to farmers markets all the time, the beach, parks, picnics, and BBQs. Our lives were normal for once and I could leave my door unlocked at night without having to worry. The whole family mellowed out and got into a new way of life and experienced happiness for the first time in a long time.

Troy decided to get a divorce and got started on it right away. I was worried what would become of me, but I knew Troy wouldn't just toss me aside. After talking we decided that when I turned eighteen he would adopt me. As far as he was concerned I was already one of his.

When school started again I was perfectly fine. The first day as I stood in line to sign in, a tall lanky looking chick was bickering and talking with her mom. I thought about introducing myself later. After I signed in I went to the gym and she was just standing there looking around. She complimented me on the Ankh symbol I wear on a chain around my neck. We started to chat and soon found out we had quite a bit in common. Her name was Christine.

I love Christine; she's a great friend. She won't let things get her down and she won't let them get you down, either. She'll give you a hug for no reason. We soon gathered more friends like Breanna, Shauna, Marcie, Ryan and Jairin who are all funny, loving, a little strange, energetic, creative, and friendly. There are lots of other people in our group that are good friends, too. With all these friends, my problems have melted away. My heart and soul are floating in joy and I feel loved for the first time in my life. Without them, I wouldn't have been able to succeed, not only in dealing with my problems, but in my everyday life as well. Just like I always say, "You can't love someone without the fear of losing them," and every day I fear losing them and never seeing them again.

My best improvement over the past year and a half is that my grades went from Fs and Ds to As and Bs. In six months I've only missed fourteen days of school, when before I would miss weeks at a time because I hated it so much. I'm getting all my credits caught up so I'll be ready to go to college to be a pharmacist. I still have some anxiety but only about getting my homework done and turning those Bs into As.

The divorce between Troy and Mom is now final and I turned eighteen in February. Troy will be adopting me soon and I'll be legally related to my stepsiblings. Even better, I'll be rid of my mom, her name, and have no connection to her.

Although I will have depression for the rest of my life—and problems of my own with friends moving, and guys, and feeling lonely—I know that's where life takes you. You can't change what's already happened but you can prevent it from happening again, or suck up your pride and deal with it. I had a horrible time trying to grow up, but always no matter what, people told me things would get better. I always waited and kept my hope, often cussing out my hope for not working faster. To my surprise, things did get better, and they keep on getting better, even with little bumps here and there.

I beat the odds from being an agoraphobic, suicidal, depressed maniac with no future in mind to being a happy, friendly, energetic, responsible, school-loving weirdo, and having more real friends than I've had my whole life put together. Here's what I've learned: Don't give up on your dreams and don't let life's obstacles get in your way. Don't give up hope; without hope I would have been done for a long time ago. Work at it and keep your goals placed strongly in your heart and you'll succeed in the end, one way or another.

Eighteen-year-old **Ashley Mackay** sees
many benefits from this book project.
"It's great to let people know your story,
let them know they're not alone, and to
express yourself to gain closure." Her
hobbies are drawing, painting, archery,
fashion designing, and gardening. After
finishing high school and college, Ashley plans to start a family.

MY GRANDPA IS THE
NUMBER ONE PERSON
IN MY FAMILY BECAUSE
WE THINK OF HIM AS A
HERO FOR HELPING AND
SUPPORTING OUR LIVES.
HE WAS FROM THE
PHILIPPINES SO WE CALL
HIM INGKONG, WHICH IS
FILIPINO FOR GRANDPA.

INGKONG
Paolo Del Donno

When he died my grandpa had no idea what a difference he made in my life. My story is about a person who gave my family and me more changes than anyone else. My grandpa is the number one person in my family because we think of him as a hero for helping and supporting our lives. He was from the Philippines so we call him ingkong, which is Filipino for grandpa; his name was Benjamin. He made us believe in ourselves because he took care of his three girls and his boy and he managed to be a good dad. Those children became my aunts, and that boy became my dad. When they had children, my ingkong took care of them and nurtured them as well. He yelled at us if we were in trouble at school or at home, but he was just teaching us a lesson about good behavior.

My story started on a Sunday in the middle of spring 2006. I was at my aunt's house waiting for my grandfather to come over for his blood transfusion. He was getting blood transfusions because he was getting weaker. As he got older he got wrinkles and he drank a lot of medicine and he had to get a transfusion at the hospital every Sunday. But for me he was a strong man because he could walk on his own, he gardened, and he was a loving and caring grandfather.

We were all watching and waiting for him to come. When we finally saw him outside, everyone was surprised that he was being carried out of the car by my uncle. My cousin Ashley went outside to help, and then everyone helped. Tita (aunt) Ming asked my uncle Bop Boy what happened. He didn't know and he just said that my grandfather had collapsed on the floor. So we put it aside and kept visiting Tita Ming, and every day Grandpa was getting weaker. The next day my mom and I were on our way home then my mom answered the phone. When she put it down I asked her who was it. "It was Bop Boy," she said. "He told me that Ingkong couldn't walk anymore because he has gotten weaker."

We went straight home to put our stuff away and then went straight to where he was. When we got there and saw Ingkong, he kept on yelling, "I want to move! I want to move!" We all stood up and group-hugged him to calm him down. "Let all your anger out," said Tita Ming. We all held a part of his body and then started crying. By ten o'clock my cousins couldn't handle our grandpa's suffering, so they decided that we had to take him to the hospital. So my cousin Ashley called Swedish Hospital to pick him up. Ashley, Megan, John, and the other cousins went outside to wait for the ambulance. I brought a box of Kleenex and went outside; it wasn't for me, it was for them because I know how emotional they are.

They started crying and kept saying to remember the good old times about Grandpa. "I am not even that emotional about this problem," I said.

"What, you mean that you don't care about our grandpa?" they said.

"No, it's not like that," I said. "I'm not crying because it's not like he's going to die or anything. I'm saving my tears for when he dies because I know he's strong enough to survive." But they kept on crying.

When the ambulance came the emergency medical technician went in the house. He asked my grandfather about his health. I couldn't actually hear because I was outside and it was crowded inside. They took him in the ambulance and went off. We all went to where he was to check and see if he was okay. For the next few weeks we kept on going to Swedish Hospital after school. Every day, we'd go to Grandpa's room, where he was resting peacefully. My aunts helped and comforted him by bringing a priest who is a dear friend to our family to pray for him. I stayed in the waiting room most of the time because of the TV and because the room was mostly crowded with people. I felt really concerned about my grandfather but I could just visit him in his room once a day because of all the family.

The doctors tried to figure out what was wrong with him. Then the doctor found a tumor in his brain. We already knew that he had cancer, but our family members had never told him about the cancer because we didn't want to worry him. So we only told him about surgery for the brain tumor.

One day, my family and I were looking for a parking space at the hospital when all of a sudden my dad got a phone call. My aunt told him that Grandpa needed him because he found out about the cancer. Even though we all took turns sleeping and staying with Grandpa, my dad is the only son that my grandpa had. So my parents insisted on having a turn sleeping in Grandpa's room. My parents decided to stay in the hospital because my aunts had to go to work.

Then our grandpa went into surgery. When we found out he had a successful surgery everything was a bit happier. But a week later he went into a coma and everyone was worried that he was going to die. In the middle of the afternoon my cousins went to buy some stuff at Bartell Drugs, my mom was helping my little brother go potty, and my dad and sister and I were in the waiting room doing nothing. Suddenly my uncle came out to the waiting room to tell my dad that Ingkong had died. All three of us went into shock. We went in the room and saw that my aunts were crying. My sister and dad went inside and I just stood outside looking all sad. Then my mom came and said, "What's wrong?" I didn't say anything so my mom pushed me aside and went inside and started crying and yelling out, "Ingkong! Ingkong!" My uncle called my cousins and they rushed in and they just burst into tears. Then I started crying.

I cried too after that, and we stayed with him for thirty minutes telling ourselves that we had taken care of him. The nurse came in to take him away and we all left with sadness.

When he died on May 15, everyone changed, even me after two or three days.

We went to see him in a casket in the Philippines. I thought to myself, I'm going back to my country for the first time. I told myself that I would try to get good grades because I keep on getting Cs and Ds. Now I get Bs and Cs, and I refuse to fight with anyone in my school because I don't want to get expelled.

I'm proud of what my ingkong did to change me in his death, because of all the yelling and the lessons about behavior. Now that he's gone I think of myself as an important person in the family. Another thing I learned was responsibility, thanks to my dear grandfather. My family is now proud of my grades. And if they keep getting better I can go to college and be a video game designer, because that's the only job for a gamer fan.

Everything changed in my life and I like it. I hope my grandpa is proud of me too…up there in heaven.

"Runner" and "television fan" are words that fourteen-year-old **Paolo Del Donno** uses to describe himself. He enjoys collecting video games, says his family inspires him, and hopes to go to college. He thinks it's "really cool" to be part of this book project.

WHEN HIS MOM TOLD
HIM THAT HIS BROTH-
ER DIED...DEMARKIS
CHANGED IN A WAY. HE
WAS MORE VIOLENT AND
DISTURBED BY LITTLE
THINGS.

So Young, So Ruthless
Deondre Simons

There was a kid named Demarkis Barks. He was a pretty much a normal kid. He had a seventeen-year-old brother named Lavonte. Demarkis got okay grades, had friends, didn't get into trouble all the time. Until one night his brother got murdered along a street in the central part of Seattle. Demarkis was fourteen years old when that happened. Now let me get into the story. Here's what happened.

Lavonte was from a gang in his area. The gang was called deuce8 folks. It happened on a summer night, around ten-thirty. His brother and three other homeboys were posted on the block. Then, next thing you know, a black SUV, driving kind of slow, skirted up from around the corner, pulled out the chopper and started letting off. Everybody hit the ground and covered their heads. The car sped off and hit the corner. After the car left, everybody got back up to their feet except Lavonte. He was shot. They called the ambulance and the ambulance took him to the hospital.

Demarkis was already tripping that his brother got shot, but that next morning he was really tripping. They thought he was going to live, but real early the next morning the doctors called his house and told their mom that Lavonte had died. When his mom told him that his brother died, Demarkis flipped. He started throwing stuff and he socked the wall and all kinds of stuff. That day, Demarkis changed in a way. He was more violent and disturbed by little things.

After that incident is when Demarkis got ruthless. He didn't care about anybody or anything. He got kicked out of his high school for things like fighting, robbing, and smoking. He even got sent to a drug and alcohol class. Demarkis would drink and smoke weed on a daily basis. He kicked it with the homies, the hood, and everything. After a while he got put on the gang. The next step he took was getting money on the block. He copped a burner from his brother's closet. It was a .38 caliber, so if you had a beef you'd have to kill the guy, because if you got caught slipping, you're dead and gone.

The first time he got booked, he was fifteen. He was charged with selling drugs and possession of a gun. He didn't get a long sentence, because it was his first offense. He got three years in juvenile and two in the county jail. It was gully in there, man. You couldn't do anything or you'd get hours. The guards were bastards. They would make fun of you in your cell, and you couldn't even put your shirt over the light at night when it was time to go to sleep. Both jails were greasy and grimy, especially the county. People would fight in the yard almost every day. There were a lot of beefs, too. There were different gangs in there, so that made even more static. He couldn't wait to get out and get back on the streets.

One summer, about five years later, he finally got out of the county. Man, everything seemed different to him. He was happy to get out and he couldn't wait to get back to his hood, his area. When he got up to deuce8 there were some new, younger members who didn't really know who he was, but the older members were excited to see him. There was a guy that sold all kinds of burners, for about $300 each. He gave Demarkis a .22 cal for free because it wasn't that big of a gun.

The first get-out gift was some cream. The older Gs gave him some cream to get on with some money. Man, in his mind everything was going his way. But there was a big beef going on between his gang and another gang called the Crips. They shot one of the first generation members from deuce8 folks, which was basically the leader because they created the hood. As the beef grew and times got harder and the years went by, more and more gang members were being killed, most of them under the age of twenty-five. Now, that's crazy.

The beef was getting deep and Demarkis was getting tired of fighting with the Crips. He was fed up with those guys. So he went to his mom's house, got $200 he'd stashed in his old room, and went to talk to the guy who was selling the burners. He told the dude that he needed a gun that spits bullets, and the dude gave him a Tech 9 with an extra clip. When he got it, he told his homeboy from when he was young to take him to the Southend into the Crips territory at night. Time passed, and the sun went down; he was ready. He went to a store and bought some masks for him and his homeboy to put on. When they got down to the spot where the Crips kick it, they were fifteen to twenty deep. At this point, no thoughts were going through his mind but to kill his enemies. So they got out of the car and ran over to the spot and sprayed everybody over there from young to old with the Tech 9. Then they ran back to the car and skirted off to his homie's house. The next morning it was on the news, but he didn't care how much of a massacre they thought it was; he was happy.

He stayed in the house for three weeks just to keep it on the low. When he finally left his house, everybody knew what had happened. What he did got around so fast that almost every gang in the Central and the Southend knew about it. That meant everybody was after his head.

About two months later, he was shot three times: once in his left thigh and twice in the back. One of those shots hit his spine. Demarkis was in the hospital for about two weeks before he died.

"Smart and cool"—these are the words fourteen-year-old **Deondre Simons** uses to describe himself. He enjoys playing basketball and kicking it with friends. One of Deondre's goals is to graduate from high school.

DIM, CLOUDY, AND BLURRY
WOULD PROBABLY
DESCRIBE MY MIND AT
THAT TIME. I PICTURED
STATIC ON THE TV.

Two Hundred and Three Million (and Me!)

Adrian Bram

The 50th anniversary of Pearl Harbor wasn't just any day. It was the day I was born: December 7, 1991. I arrived early in the morning in Maryville, Missouri, just before the time the attack occurred in Hawaii. My mom, Tina, told me that for the whole year, everyone was talking about the anniversary in my hometown of 10,600 people.

I learned how to read between the ages of three and four years old. By the time I was in first grade I was reading at a fifth-grade level, according to the school and the stories my mom tells. When I was in second grade the first Harry Potter book came out, and I read the whole thing. I did have trouble reading out loud, but I could breeze through words on the page in my head.

When I was young, my dad, Jeff, ran a funeral home. Every night I would get up and try to find the bathroom, which was down a creepy hallway. There were caskets down the hall. I always made it past them, sometimes holding my teddy bear.

I remember being made fun of in school. I have Tourette's syndrome. I didn't curse a lot, which they expected me to, but I did have tics—I shrugged my shoulders, locked up my elbows, and made sounds. I don't remember much because medications blurred my memory. I took several types. I took anti-psychotics, an anti-seizure drug, and an anti-depressant. They were all mind-altering. Dim, cloudy, and blurry would probably describe my mind at that time. I pictured static on the TV.

In kindergarten, I was in the classroom only 10 percent of the time. I was always in the office, or was sent home. I was always in trouble. One time the principal jerked me into his office physically. He yanked on my shirt, and basically threw me into the office. I don't remember anything else about that day.

In 1994, when I was three years of age, my sister Jessica was born on January 1. At about that time, my parents, who had never married, split up. I lived with mom. Later, Dad got custody, and we lived in the country near a farm. I remember going mushroom hunting. We collected them and brought them home for dinner. I remember a picture of my aunts holding up giant mushrooms.

In 1999, my mom moved to Seattle with my older brother, Anthony. In 2000, I came to Seattle to visit them. I came back in 2003, and we went up in the Space Needle for the first time. I got lightheaded up at the top, and we had to go back down. This was the year that my stepdad came into the picture. I visited again one more time for one month with my sister in 2006.

My mom wanted me to live in Seattle. We had to go to court to have a judge decide if I could move to Seattle. I had stomach ulcers because I was so nervous about it. The judge asked me what I preferred to do, and I said that I wanted to move to Seattle. I couldn't really understand what the judge's decision was until the lawyer said, "He said yes, you can go to Seattle."

So in August 2006 I moved to Seattle. I flew here on the airplane with just my laptop for company. Now, I live with my mom and stepdad, and my little sister Aya, who is two years old. I live in an apartment in Northgate. I can walk to Safeway and get some food, instead of having to drive twenty miles. I used to ride in a yellow school bus; now I take Metro.

At my school in Seattle, I haven't been made fun of as much as I was in Missouri. I still have Tourette's, though, and it is unpleasant. I have neck and head tics. But I am making friends. There are a lot more people to meet. The new people have taught me a lot. I learn something every day. I picture the mind as stuffed full of glue. The mind is malleable. Every time we learn something, our brain glue becomes unstuck, and our brain expands.

I'm really glad I moved to Seattle. I needed a fresh start. I like my school, but I think I will try to transfer somewhere else next year. It will be another change, but I feel like I'm ready for it. Moving to Seattle and getting off of my medications have made me feel much better. I can think much more clearly and adapt to changes better.

Fifteen-year-old **Adrian Bram** is inspired by his mother and father and plans on following in the footsteps of his older brother. He enjoys working with computers and says he has "good experience with technology."

THEN ONE DAY I THOUGHT
ABOUT CHANGING AND
STOPPING ALL THE BAD
STUFF THAT MESSED UP
MY LIFE. SCHOOL WAS
THE FIRST THING I KNEW
I WAS MESSING UP.

Don't Fade Away
Lemara Vaiese

I'm half Samoan and half Filipino and the youngest in a family of three brothers and one sister. I have changed and learned a lot over the past few years of my life, especially as a teenager. I think differently now about my priorities, friends, school, and attitude. It's hard for me to even explain.

My childhood was going really good. I always used to go outside, play ball, and just run for fun. I used to be really happy all the time. Then my life changed because of drugs and alcohol. I got into a lot of trouble because it started messing up my brain. I couldn't think straight and my body was weak. I became a big troublemaker. I thought drugs were cool, but not anymore. They did a lot of damage to me.

When I was in the seventh grade at Eckstein, I got into smoking with my friends. I started drinking the year after that. The crowd of people I hung out with also smoked and drank.

In eighth grade I did my research project on nicotine, which is the stuff in cigarettes that makes smoking addictive. I learned that nicotine in cigarettes makes smokers want to buy a carton of smokes every day. People realize that smoking is really bad for their health, but they still do it. When I was little, my mom told me a story about how my grandfather died of smoking. Smoking is really addictive and my grandfather smoked every day. I don't want that to happen to my people or me.

I continued using drugs and alcohol at Nathan Hale High School with my old and new friends. Then one day I thought about changing and stopping all the bad stuff that messed up my life. School was the first thing I knew I was messing up. I skipped classes and sometimes a whole day of school. My grades were dropping and I didn't want to go to class at all. I wondered what the point was of going to class when I was failing.

Things really changed on the day of October 19th, 2006. That's the day when I got laced up with some PCP (angel dust) when I was chiefing, which is a term for smoking marijuana. I went through some exorcism stuff that's hard to explain, like me talking but nothing coming out of my mouth. I was really cold and sweating at the same time, and dizzy. I almost blacked out. After a few hours, I threw up black stuff. I felt so weak. I didn't feel right. I didn't feel like myself.

Before I started using drugs and alcohol, I was happy and cheerful inside. Now I don't really remember my teenage years. I don't remember what I did every day, like my past has already started to fade away.

The thing is, I'm trying to send a message to all you teenagers out there. Drugs, smoking, and alcohol are really bad for you. It's not a good thing to do when you're growing up. Drugs and alcohol can kill you. I don't want to die.

"I think that this project is great," says seventeen-year-old **Lemara Vaiese**. She considers herself funny, outgoing, happy, and cool. Lemara's hobbies are basketball and music, and right now her goal is to finish high school.

I DID NOT WANT TO DO
THIS ALL OVER AGAIN.
I WAS SCARED. I WAS
MOVING EVEN FARTHER
AWAY FROM MY MOM AND
FAMILY AND FRIENDS.

The Way Moving Affects My Life
Tallon Johnson

I have moved a lot in my life. Hard times have come and gone, but I have found my way through it all. My mom is a single mother with three children and one job. She has tried her best at everything she has done. We have moved from state to state, city to city, and house to house. We have moved to get away from things or just to start over new.

When I was ten years old we moved to Fort Walton Beach, Florida, to start a new life and to get away from our problems. I loved it there. Friends and I always got to hang out at the beach. We went to water parks, we went fishing, and life was great. I loved to make new friends but one thing always popped into my head: Are we going to move again?

I came home from school one day and opened the door to see my mom packing. Boxes were all over the room. I was confused. I was finally happy and was comfortable with where I lived. I dropped my backpack and asked my mom, "What are you doing? Where are we going? What happened?" So many questions were going through my head at that moment.

My mom turned her head to answer me, "We're moving to Las Vegas." I didn't know what to think. I trusted my mom, so we had to be moving for a good reason.

"Why are we moving?" I asked.

"We are moving because your aunt Nina wants us to, and she said she can help us get back on our feet."

My mom is not as fortunate as many parents are. Sometimes we have had a hard time. My mom has tried her best. We weren't able to go shopping whenever we wanted to because we had priorities. We had to pay the bills, try to fix the car, and get food. I was only twelve years old at that time and I didn't know how to react.

On our way to Las Vegas I was stressed, and I was mad. I didn't talk to my mom the whole way there. After four days of driving through several states, we finally arrived in Las Vegas. It looked all right. I was sort of scared because of the people I saw, and the things that they were doing like tagging, selling drugs, etc. I felt left out, and worried that I wasn't going to fit in. As my mom and I arrived at my aunt's house, we got out of the car and headed for the door. The house was huge, and it was bright. I felt safe. My mom rang the doorbell, and as my aunt opened the door, she welcomed us into the house. I already felt comfortable there.

I started school about three weeks after we arrived. The first day at school went great. I met a lot of people, but one particular girl, Jenna, was great and she was really friendly and really sweet. I knew when we started to talk we would be best friends because we had so much in common. We liked the same type of music, wore the same style of clothes, and we both loved to sing. Jenna helped me in school and showed me around. She always told me to "never be scared of the people around you, just be scared of the surroundings that they bring with them." I didn't understand her at first but now I know what she was talking about.

The school is an arts academy, K.O. Knudson Middle School. It was great. In sixth grade I was in choir. I had so much fun in that class. We performed about six times a year. I love to sing. It is my life. I think I get my voice from my mom, who is a wonderful singer. In seventh and eighth grade I was in dance. I took that class because it sounded like fun, but I thought wrong. It was difficult. I wanted to quit and I almost did until my dance teacher told me, "If you quit, you're a quitter."

After she told me that, I thought about it. I love to succeed in everything I do. I went back to class the next day, and I spoke to her. I told her, "I don't want to quit. I want to stay."

She looked at me with a bright smile on her face and said, "I was hoping you would come back." After that day I knew I could never quit anything that I do.

Las Vegas was great and I had a great life there. Everything that happens to a teenage girl happened to me in Vegas. I was in love for the first time, I got into trouble sometimes, my heart was broken, and I was cheated on. Even though these things happened to me, I believe I found myself. As I entered my teens, my attitude began to change. Instead of having my own style, I began to dress like everyone else. I started to talk with a Las Vegas slang, and my personality began winding up. I was bubbly, energetic, and I talked a lot. I am grateful for the people I hung out with then and the environment I was in, because if I hadn't had those experiences I wouldn't be the person that I am today.

Everything was going great, but my mom was frustrated with Las Vegas and bad things began to happen: gangs around our house, drive-bys, killings, break-ins, and drama. I was going through a lot. I was in love with a boy who treated me like crap, I was doing horrible in school, I found out my grandma had breast cancer, and last but not least, we were moving again.

It was terrible. I wanted to stay for a birthday party for one of my close friends. My mom let me. I lived with my mom's friend Jessica. She helped me through a lot. She bought me clothes, fed me break-fast, lunch, and dinner, and let me hang out with my friends whenever I wanted to. My life was going great, but time was going by fast, and I didn't have much time left. I had about two weeks.

My aunt Vicky called Jessica and was talking to her about something. I had no idea what. I began to feel nervous. As Jessica hung up the phone, she looked at me with an upset face, which made me feel uncomfortable. "Your aunt called and told me that she wants to take you to live with her in Hawaii." I didn't know what to say. I was confused. I asked Jessica why my aunt wanted me to move in with her and she said, "Your mother is going through a hard time right now." After she told me what happened, I called my mom. I told her everything that happened and she was not happy at all. My mom wanted to fly me out to Seattle right away, but my aunt wanted me to stay with her for about a year. So I did.

For the next week I packed my belongings. I did not want to do this all over again. I was scared. I was moving even farther away from my mom and family and friends. I was going to a new place. We began to drive to my ex's house to drop me off to hang out with him for a little bit before I had to go catch my plane to Hawaii. We arrived at his house and I started to cry. I couldn't believe I was actually saying goodbye to the one person I loved. I knocked on his door and he answered. I looked at him with tears running down my cheeks. He didn't say one word to me. He wrapped his arms around me and held me tight until I stopped crying. When I finally stopped crying he invited me inside his cozy house. We sat down at the dinner table and we talked about the good times.

"Remember when you accidentally pushed me into the pond that one cold day?" I said.

"Yeah, I remember that, wow, funny times."

As he talked some more I thought to myself, "I can't believe this is really happening." A knock at the door interrupted my thought. I knew it was the time for me to say goodbye forever. I started to head for the door. He opened it for me and stood by the door.

"I will always remember you, Adalberto, and I will never forget you," I said as I wrapped my arms around his waist and held him so tight. He did the same.

"Don't do anything stupid, Tallon, and stay out of trouble and always remember I will always care for you."

Those were the feelings I had been waiting to hear from him. I walked to the car door not looking back. My mom had always told me, "Never look back when you say your goodbyes." I never understood that either until I finally took her word for it. I didn't look back.

Jessica drove me to the airport and we waited with my aunt Nina and my cousin Chris and more family and friends. "Oahu, Hawaii boarding up!" Those words made me mad. I didn't want to leave, I didn't want to say goodbye to the ones I loved, and I didn't want to move again. I went on the plane, found my seat, and began to cry. I never thought that leaving Las Vegas would affect me like this. Not Las Vegas itself, but the people who live there.

I arrived at the Oahu airport and saw my aunt standing there with my uncle and my cousin Kayleigh. She was so cute and little.

We headed for the car. My uncle put my luggage into the back of the car. As we drove around the island I noticed that everything was peaceful. The things that caught my eye were the beautiful mountains, the dark blue, shiny ocean, and all the plants around me. It was a wonderful night to arrive in Hawaii. I could tell I was going to love it.

Two weeks passed and I was on my way to high school. Radford High School had a great football team and national championship cheerleaders who were also great. The school was okay but it was not the same as the schools I was accustomed to.

As time went on I noticed that my aunt began to come down hard on me when it came to school. I understood what she wanted me to do, but it became frustrating and she knew I was getting annoyed with her harping on me all the time. School is very important to her. She wants me to have a great job and to be successful. My aunt is a good person who cares for me and wants me to do my best. That was the only thing holding me back from giving up.

School was frustrating and I was ready for a long break. Finally winter break arrived. I was so excited. I was going to go see my mom for Christmas. I got on the plane to Seattle. It took a while but I finally made it. I got off the plane and I saw my mom waiting for me. I started to cry. I was so happy that I finally got to be in my mom's arms and got to feel her warm arms around my body. Right then I knew I was home. We got my luggage and went to Starbucks. I was so tired I needed some caffeine in me. When we got to the house I found my two little brothers playing video games just like old times. The weather was cold. I knew then Seattle's weather was not like Hawaii's.

Christmas morning came. Everyone was happy and cheerful, which was very unusual because my family is not a morning family. We all opened our presents and gave each other hugs and kisses—all the loving family stuff. But it was heartwarming to know I have a family whose members will hug me and kiss me just because they care.

My aunt called me on my new cell phone a few days after Christmas and asked me, "Do you want to stay there with your mom?"

I didn't know what to say. I thought if I said yes she would get upset at me even though she was the one asking me. And if I said no, my mom would hate me. I put all that aside and thought about my options. Finally I came up with an answer for my aunt. "Yes, Aunt Vicky, I want to stay. Not because I know my mom would be happy but because I think it would be good for me." My aunt didn't say anything to indicate she was upset at me but in her voice I knew she was upset because she wanted me to stay with her.

Finally, I was home. It was great to be with my mom and feel relaxed. My brother and I started at John Marshall Alternative School. I was scared about this school. I had heard a lot of rumors, including that every day people would fight over stupid things and would cuss out the teachers. But as I got to all my ninth-grade classes and I began to meet nice people, I found out those rumors are not true. I grew to like this school. My brother and I feel comfortable here. The teachers are great and the students are funny and nice. I love Seattle.

So far my life has been like a movie. It has had drama, a crisis, and a solution. When I have seen something wrong, I have tried to revise it and get it right. It's an ongoing process.

Thankfully, there's one question that doesn't pop into my head anymore: Are we going to move again? I know that I am home now and I know who I am now. I have gone through a lot but I think that is why I am the person I am today.

"I love to make people laugh," says fifteen-year-old **Tallon Johnson**. "I am never boring." Tallon is most inspired by her mother, who, she says, "is a strong woman I can always count on to be there for me." Tallon enjoys dancing, singing, hanging out with friends, and teaching, and she plans to attend college.

THEY CALL US THE
MINORITY WHEN REALLY
WE ARE MOST OF THIS
COUNTRY.

Bottom of the Food Chain
Sthefano Esteves

9/11 was a big change for immigrants in the United Sates. Since the attack happened, the government has been a little paranoid about letting people into this country. My homeboy Ricardo speaks of this as if it is a religion to him; it's really more important to him than anything else. It affected his family so much that it put them at the bottom of the food chain.

He was thirty-one years old, living by himself in Miami, with family in Guatemala to support on his back when 9/11 happened. At the moment Ricardo was making some deal with his cousin Luis, who lived in Guatemala and was planning on coming here to work. Ricardo had sent Luis $3,000 to get his paperwork done. He had to get his passport, a visa, and his airline ticket. Luis had all that done and was going to fly out of Guatemala on September 19, 2001. But because of 9/11, he couldn't fly out and all the money was lost.

Ricardo was sad for what happened, but didn't let it set him back. He kept on working to save his money like he did before. But a couple of weeks after 9/11, the government got a little paranoid and decided that if it was that easy for terrorists to come to the country, that maybe it needed to come up with the plan to stop immigrants coming as well, in case they are terrorists, too. Ricardo was out of the job and had to use his savings for a whole month. He then got a job as a server, when before he worked as a chef for the Marriott Hotel. He went economically low, but he had to do it to keep going.

It got harder. People kept checking to see if he had a real Social Security number. His jobs would only last for a matter of months or even weeks. He told me, "Not having papers makes things difficult in this country."

9/11 was a problem for every immigrant here because the government made a law that if you don't check documentation for the employee's Social Security number or for anything that makes him eligible to work in the U.S., it means you are helping immigrants and that's a fine in some states. So it got harder. Many people had so many money problems. Many families ended up moving to other states where they heard immigrants lived better. States like Minnesota, Idaho, Washington, Oregon, Utah, and more. States that don't call out too much attention are states like California, Illinois, Indiana, New York, and Florida.

Before 9/11, Ricardo made about sixteen dollars an hour, but after 9/11 it was cut in half and, minus taxes, it killed Ricardo's paycheck. Ricardo had to move from Miami to Seattle. It was a tough move for him, but he has a job that has been working out for him for the past two and a half years. Ricardo is doing a lot better now, but his cousin is still stuck in Guatemala with the rest of his family.

The consequences would be very serious if this country were to end up without immigrants. Culture would be missed. This country is made of other countries put together; it doesn't have its own traditions, foods, music, celebrations, and more. What would this country be without people from other countries? I'm not only talking about

Hispanics, I'm talking about the whole globe, like Italians, Germans, Greeks, Australians, Chinese, and many more. So if they really wanted us out they would lose a lot of money.

Celebrations like St. Patrick's Day, Cinco De Mayo, and Chinese New Year, are some examples of holidays Americans enjoy. They call us the minority when really we are most of this country. I think the best thing they can do is make it easier for us, and turn us all into legal aliens, or residents.

In the years after 9/11 I saw a lot of change in this country, and not for the better. I saw a lot of people get deported, families suffering, and relatives getting shipped off to their countries. Watching this changed the way I think about this country; everyone had made look like it was a dream to be here, but seeing this happen made me realize that life is hard.

Seventeen-year-old **Sthefano Esteves**
would describe himself as brave, but it's
his sense of humor that he likes most
about himself. He is inspired by his
family, and he hopes one day to have his
own, along with a career. What are his
thoughts about this book project? "It's
a good idea to get students' stories out
to see how this century is different than
before."

I'M ONLY ONE PERSON.
I CAN ONLY BE ME. NO
ONE CAN SIT THERE
AND TELL ME TO
CHANGE MY WAYS. I'M
NOT GOING TO CHANGE
FOR ANYONE ELSE BUT
MYSELF.

People Don't Change, Things Change People
Christina Nguyen

Change: To make the form, nature, content, future course, etc., of (something) different from what it is or from what it would be if left alone.

Change can sometimes be a good thing, but not always. A lot of people come and go in my life. It's nothing new. Everyone has flaws and no one is perfect but I don't trust just anyone because not everyone is trustworthy. One minute someone may say she is a friend. Then the next minute she talks about you as if she always hated you. And, all of a sudden, she's spreading your business to everyone. I understand that some people are going to have something bad to say about you. Most people want to believe a lie, but then again, deny the truth.

I always say I'm going to change in some way even though I realize you can't change who you really are. I told myself I was going to cut everyone off because they couldn't do anything for me. I can be independent, but in this world you have to depend on someone in some way. I guess I just have to choose my friends wisely and keep them at a certain distance. In this world, you are the one who knows you best.

When I was in middle school I couldn't lie, but I was an instigator because I just love drama. Everyone warned me about high school and said I shouldn't get caught up in it. I decided to stay out of other people's business. I told myself that if I were to hear something about another person I would just keep it to myself because I knew if I started to run my mouth I would be caught up in the middle.

You always learn from your mistakes. When I watch other people talking about "she said this, she said that," it gets annoying and shows ignorance. I feel like I'm smarter than that and I have better things to do besides running around yelling and screaming. I don't want to come off as uneducated and unladylike. Drama is not the way to go. It's entertaining and everything but if you're a part of it, there's nothing entertaining about it.

When I first got to West Seattle High School I decided it was time to start fresh. I barely knew anyone there and I liked that. No one could talk about me because no one knew me. I knew just a couple people and they were juniors and seniors while I was only a freshman.

I finally met new people at the school, but I didn't know what I was getting myself into. I met a girl named Cheryl. She was cool. She knew I was not the type to run my mouth about anyone, so she told me everything. She talks a lot of mess because she has a lot of cousins who go there and she knows they've got her back. She talks about everyone and I was getting tired of hearing her mess. I tried to stay away from her.

When I tried to keep to myself, people kept coming up to me and telling me what they heard about me. Clearly, I had something they didn't. Everyone was just mad at me because I didn't want to talk to anyone about drama. When I sat there and someone was talking about someone, I just walked away because I didn't want to hear about anyone. I got sidetracked when Charlie was talking to me about Cheryl. Charlie is one of Cheryl's cousins. I wanted to know more about what Charlie was talking about so I called Cheryl.

"Cheryl, I heard you were beefin' with Tyler."

"Yeah, I don't like that girl. She's mad because I kissed Jerry."

Jerry is the guy Charlie messes with but they weren't officially going out.

"Well, didn't Sissy kiss him too?" I asked.

"That's what I'm talking about. They going around calling me yuk mouth but Sissy kissed him after me and Charlie."

The next day at school I just had to go and run my mouth to Sissy and told her that Cheryl asked why they call her yuk mouth and not Sissy. I thought I wasn't gonna get caught up. Damn, was I wrong. When Sissy went up to Cheryl and asked her why she was talking mess, Cheryl wanted to start lying, saying she never said that but clearly I was on the phone when she said it. I was getting irritated. So was Sissy, because Cheryl was lying to both of us. Sissy was about to knock her dome in. Everyone was getting her too excited. Everyone kept saying she wouldn't do anything but it looked like she was ready to steal on her until the teacher came.

Later we were all in the Teen Life Center. Everyone who was involved in the whole situation was yelling at one another. Half were blaming me for running my mouth while the other half of us were blaming Cheryl for saying anything in the first place just because she has a lot of people who have her back. In the end we all lost. I got what I wanted: being a loner. But not how I imagined it. I wanted to be cool with everyone and still not talk to anyone but instead everyone hated me and I'm still a loner.

I learned a lot from that day. There are some things I should just keep to myself. I have changed my ways. When I hear things now I don't go running my mouth to the next person, repeating what I heard so I get caught up. Never again.

Who is anyone to tell me what I should and shouldn't do? What I can and can't say? Who is anyone to tell me whom I can and can't hang out with or talk to? Why do you care? I have learned to ask myself questions like that. Just because you don't like someone doesn't always mean everyone else has to hate them as well.

I'm only one person. I'm only me. I can only be me. No one can sit there and tell me to change my ways. I'm not going to change for anyone else but myself. If people can't handle the fact that I can only be myself and not what everyone expects me to be, then they're really not worth my time.

Now I'm in the tenth grade at John Marshall Alternative School. I'm just trying to get through school. I'm not worried about anyone or anything except my education. Once in a while, I'll get caught up but then I stop and remind myself of the real reason I'm here. I have changed since last year. I'm not running my mouth and I just keep things to myself because you never know when you could be saying the wrong thing to the wrong person.

"A great opportunity." This is how fifteen-year-old **Christina Nguyen** feels about this book project. She considers herself outgoing, and she is inspired by herself and her mother. Her hobbies include reading and kicking it, and she plans on finishing school.

I THINK THAT WHATEVER
HAPPENED IN THE PAST
STAYS IN THE PAST. I
JUST GET GHOST.

Moving Forward Like a Chevy
Anthony D. Vaughn

The big changes that I have gone through came from changing schools. I'm in eighth grade and have been to five different schools so far. I went to Rainier View from kindergarten through second grade. I left this school because a sex offender moved into a house right next to the school. I switched to Emerson Elementary, which was also in my neighborhood. The first day at Emerson, I was assigned to a table group and they showed me around the school. The other kids in my table group became my friends, and I made other friends at that school, including my best friend, Kwame. I call Kwame my brother and I call his sister, Imani, my sister. I stayed at Emerson from third to fifth grade, until the end of elementary school.

Next, I went to Hamilton International Middle School. Hamilton was far from my house, so I had to get up at 6:00 a.m. and ride on a school bus for forty-five minutes. I didn't mind, though, because I had lots of friends that rode that bus. I liked Hamilton. The principal was nice and would say, "What's up, my brotha?" I knew him before I went to Hamilton because he worked at the summer camp I went to the summer after fifth grade. Kwame went to Hamilton, and it was fun to go to school with my best friend. My favorite class was math because I was good at it. I especially like fractions. I thought my other classes were boring because I was not interested in them. Sometimes I would talk in class when I was not supposed to, but I was not a big troublemaker.

Even though I liked Hamilton, I decided to try a different school, McClure Middle School, for seventh grade. I was hearing from other people that McClure was a good school. I liked McClure. There were kids there from my elementary school, so I made friends easily there, too.

McClure had a rule where you could only go to the school dances if you turned in all of your work. At the end of the school year, I turned in all of my work like I was supposed to, and I went to the dance. I don't know why, but the teacher that was chaperoning the dance didn't believe that I turned in all of my work. After I was at the dance for about twenty minutes, she just came out of nowhere and pushed me. I went back to the classroom where I had turned my work in, and the teacher there showed her the work. I think she felt dumb, but she didn't apologize.

I felt humiliated, but I went back to the dance even though I didn't feel like it. I called my mom when school was out, and she came to the school. I got a refund for the dance and my mom called the police. Nothing happened to the teacher, but she was polite to me for the rest of the year. My mom and I decided that it would be best for me to go back to Hamilton.

I went back to Hamilton for eighth grade and everything was going fine. The only problem was that none of the teachers liked that I would speak up for myself or that I spoke up for other kids. In January, my science teacher and my social studies teacher were cheating me out of my grade. On one multiple-choice test in science, I got an

F. I could see that she had erased my correct answers, so I went to the principal and he corrected the test for me. I got 100 percent on that test. I couldn't do anything about the social studies grade, but it made me not want to go to that school anymore. So in February I came to my current school, John Marshall.

John Marshall has kids who are here for a lot of different reasons, but it feels a lot the same to me as my other schools. The big difference here is that there are high school students along with middle school. I knew some of the kids already when I came here and even though I have only been here for a month, I've already made friends with everyone in my class. The teachers at this school treat me with respect, so there's no problem.

In the summertime, I am planning to move to another city near Seattle called Federal Way. My uncle lives there, and he says that the schools there are better than they are in Seattle. Because of everything that's happened to me at the schools in Seattle, my mom, my uncle, and I decided that going to a better school district would be the best thing.

I'm not sure yet which school I will be going to. It's my goal to stay at the same school for all four years of high school, no matter what happens. I'll still see my friends from my neighborhood when I stay with my mom on the weekends, so it doesn't matter that I won't be going to school with them.

I think that whatever happened in the past stays in the past. I just get ghost. These school changes made me stronger and more confident. As I come face to face with more changes in life, I'm just going to deal with them, not because I want to, but because I have to. In life there is no turning back, you just have to keep moving forward, like a Chevy.

"Awesome." This is what fourteen-year-old **Anthony Vaughn** thinks about this book project. He describes himself as "a boss," and of all the things he likes about himself, he likes his attitude best. Anthony plans on becoming a CPA, and his mother and uncle inspire him.

TODAY I GOT A CALL
FROM MY COUSIN, THE
ONE WHO LIVES IN
AMERICA. SHE TELLS
ME HOW SHE'S TRYING
TO GET US TO COME
LIVE IN THE U.S. WITH
HER, BUT I DOUBT IT
WILL HAPPEN.

Diary of a Teenage Somalian
Hana Mohamed

January 13, 1988

Today is my thirteenth birthday. Mommy left for Hargeisa to visit her sick mother. "Take good care of those kids, Lalya." she said. "I'll be back in five days. Understand?"

"Okay, Mommy. Say hello to Grandma for me," I replied as I closed the door. God, I had lots of work to do before the kids woke up.

Just as I finished my chores, Abdi came running through the door. "Lalya, come here quick. Mohamed fell out of a tree."

"What?" I replied. "Why was he up a tree in the first place?"

"Me and him were seeing who could climb the highest. It was all Mohamed's idea."

I looked at Abdi with disappointment as I ran and see if Mohamed was okay. When I got there, Mohamed was lying on the cold, hard, wet ground, crying his heart out, and Sarah was screaming, as if she just saw a lion: "I think he broke his leg."

I didn't know what to do. Father was at work, Mother was at Grandmother's, and the nearest doctor was sixty miles away.

But just then, Daddy walked through the door. He looked at Mohamed, then at me, and I knew my life was over.

"How could this happen? You were supposed to watch them. How could you let them climb a tree? Answer me when I'm talking to you, Lalya," screamed Daddy.

"I'm sorry, Daddy. I didn't know what they were doing. I was cleaning up the house," I replied with tears in my eyes. I could tell Father was disappointed in me. It was entirely my fault; I was responsible for Mohamed. If only I had done my chores faster, Mohamed would have never climbed that tree and broken his leg. I felt so bad. What was I going to tell Mom when she came home? She'd be so angry with me. She'd never trust me with the kids again.

January 18, 1988

Mom is coming home today. I hope she doesn't get mad at me. I don't want her to think I'm irresponsible. God, I'm scared out of my mind. What will Mom think of me when she finds out that Mohamed broke his leg climbing a tree?

* * * * *

Mom is home now. She wasn't mad at all. She just told me to watch the kids next time and make sure I know what they're doing every second. She said we can't afford to take Mohamed to the doctor right now, because we're kind of low on money, so we're just going to let his leg heal on its own. Anyway, I have to go. I have to go grocery shopping.

March 15, 1988

I've been so busy taking care of the family. Grandma is getting sicker and sicker every day, which means more chores for me. Mommy left again and said she'd be back when Grandma gets better. The kids just went to sleep. Dad has been busy working overtime to pay for Grandma's doctor bills.

March 17, 1988

Oh my god, Grandma died this morning. Mom's devastated. I feel so sad. I didn't even get to see Grandma. I haven't seen her in years, but I'm going to miss her. Uncle Shuaib and Aunt Hawa are here visiting to see how Mom's doing, since she was the closest to Grandma. I can see the fear in their eyes. They have been praying all day for Grandma, praying that God will forgive her for the bad deeds that she may have done when she was alive.

July 4, 1988

It has been more than three months since Grandma's death, and Mom is still mourning it. She's raw-boned, colorless, dim, and terrible looking. She won't even eat anything. What should I do? I'm so afraid she will starve herself to death. I don't think she'll ever get over Grandma's death. Life seems to be going slower and slower.

September 7, 1988

The kids started school today, but I haven't gone to school since I was eleven. "You're a big girl now, Lalya," Daddy told me when he drove me home on my last day of school two years ago. "It's time for you to stay home and help your mother with the house."

Dad's right. I'm not a kid anymore. I need to help out Mommy, especially now that she just had a baby. I would still like to go to school, but I have more responsibilities now that I have a new baby brother.

January 1989

"Lalya, come here," Mommy said earlier tonight. "Your father and I have some important news for you."

"Okay, Mommy. I'll be there in a few minutes," I replied as I finished cooking dinner. When I walked through the door, I noticed Yusf and his family sitting on the couch across from my mother and father. Yusf is like family to us; he has lived across the street for six years.

"Your father and I have decided that you're old enough to start your own family," Mommy said.

"What?"

"Yes, it's time for you and Yusf to get married."

I couldn't believe what I was hearing. Were they serious?

"Lalya, what do you think of this?" asked Mom, moving closer to me. I could see the happiness in her face. I couldn't rain on her parade. But, what was I supposed to do?

"Lalya, answer your mother when she's talking to you," yelled Daddy.

"Okay. I guess it's okay, Mom." Yusf and his family jumped up and down in excitement. My mom started crying tears of joy.

January 15, 1989

I couldn't sleep all night. I kept thinking of being married to Yusf. He's such an old dirty slob. I feel like my world is coming to an end. I can't get married to that man. No! This can't be happening to me. Maybe I should just tell Mom how I feel. No, I can't. She'll hate me for the rest of my life. Oh my god, what should I do?

January 16, 1989

Everybody's talking about the wedding. It seems like they're all blind, that nobody can see how I really feel. I feel so depressed. I don't care anymore. I decided to tell Mom the truth. I couldn't deal with it anymore.

"Mommy, I'm not going to marry Yusf," I said. "I can't marry him; I won't!"

"What?" she said, looking confused.

"I'm not marrying Yusf."

"Yes, you are!"

"No, Mommy, I'm not!" I could tell that she was getting mad. "Mommy, I don't want to marry Yusf. He's grimy, lazy, and ugly. I don't want to be married to a guy like that."

"Well, too bad, because you have to."

"Mom, I'm not going to argue about this. This is my choice, and I have made my decision."

"Well, we'll see what your father thinks about that."

When Dad came home, I could hear Mom and him talking. I knew he was going to kill me. Yusf's dad is like a brother to him.

I heard Dad's footsteps coming up the stairs. "Open the door, Lalya."

"No, Daddy, I don't want to marry Yusf!"

"I don't care, just open the door."

I was so terrified that I couldn't move to open the door.

"You little rat, you have to marry Yusf! I don't care what you want and don't want," Dad screamed out as he knocked down the door.

I knew that if I talked back and didn't tell him what he wanted to hear, he'd be mad at me. So I didn't have a choice but to agree. "Okay, Daddy," I said. "I'll marry Yusf."

February 4, 1989

Yusf came by to say hello, and guess what? Mommy invited him to stay for dinner. God, I can't stand him. His face makes me want to vomit. How can a person be so disgusting looking? His pants are torn apart. His shirt has no buttons, so his hairy, creepy chest shows. He smells like dirty laundry.

I could live the rest of my life without seeing this guy again. I can't marry somebody in such disarray and so fortuneless. Yet, there's nothing I can do to change my parents' mind.

You should have seen how sloppy he was at dinner. He was eating as if he hadn't eaten anything in years. He stuffed his face with mashed potatoes, and he killed his chicken in less than a minute. How much nastier could he get?

February 8, 1989

The wedding is in two days. I can't go through with this. I feel like I'm caught in a box with no escape. You know what? I'm going to run away. I'm tired of always doing what I'm told just to make my parents happy. But if I run away, where can I go? Where can I stay?

* * * * *

I made up my mind to go to Aunt Hawa's. She's the only person in the world I can trust, and the only person who will understand to me. I sneaked out of my home late at night. It was so dark and bloodcurdling outside. I felt so abandoned, isolated, and lonely.

"Lalya, what are you doing here?" asked Aunt Hawa when I arrived at her door. I could tell she was surprised to see me.

"Auntie, I ran way from home. I couldn't stand all the pressure of getting married," I replied with my head down so I couldn't look her in the eye.

"Oh, I see. You don't want to marry Yusf, do you?"

"No, I don't," I said, closing the door behind me.

"You know what, Lalya? I went through the same thing when I was your age. My mom wanted me to marry this guy I hated, but I said, 'No.' But I didn't run away from home, because that wasn't going to solve anything. Okay?"

I knew she was right. "But I've said no, and nobody wants to listen," I replied with tears in my eyes.

"How about I talk to your parents and tell them how you feel?"

"Okay, but I don't think it will work."

"Trust me, it will work, and if it doesn't you can stay here with me as long as you like."

"Thanks," I replied as I went to the kitchen to get something to eat.

February 9, 1989

Aunt Hawa talked to Mommy and told her how I felt. And guess what? Mommy was cool with it; the wedding's off. I hope Yusf's family isn't too devastated. I hope they don't think of Yusf as a failure now.

January 13, 1990

I woke up this morning and noticed that something was different, but I couldn't put my finger on it. Dad was cheerful. Mom was calm and relaxed for a change. I said out loud to nobody in particular, "There's something different around here." My brother and sister, Abdi and Sarah, looked up but didn't say a word. So, I just forgot about it and got started with my chores.

As I finished my chores, somebody knocked on the door; I ran and opened it.

"Hi, you must be Lalya. Are your parents home?" said an older man who had a boy about three year older than me with him.

"Yeah, Dad's upstairs. I'll get him. Come and have a seat," I replied as I lead them to the living room.

After about an hour, Father called me in to tell me something. "Lalya, this is Ali," he said, pointing to the boy sitting on the couch. Ali stood up and told me a little about himself. He told me he has his own big company. Then his dad started bragging about how rich and smart his kid is. At that point, I knew something was up.

"Lalya, why don't you and Ali go take a walk or something. Your father and I have some business we have to take care of," said Ali's father, with a huge grin on his face.

I don't know how, but Ali and I spent the whole day together. He's a really neat guy and guess what? He's picking me up tomorrow so we can hang out some more.

January 14, 1990

God, I haven't had so much fun in years. Ali took me to his work, and the building was so big. After giving me a tour of his company, we went for a walk in the park. He is so sweet and kind. It seems like I've known him all my life. He is nothing like Yusf.

January 15, 1990

Turns out Ali's a fake. Our parents wanted us to get married the whole time, and he knew about it. That's the reason he was at our house in the first place. How could I have been so wrong about him?

* * * * *

I called Aunt Hawa and talked to her about the whole thing. She said that it wasn't Ali's fault, that he was just doing what his dad wanted. She said that if I like him, I should go for it.

February 14, 1990

Ali and I are getting married in two days. I can't believe this. I'm so excited. Everything has just got to be perfect. We already picked out the house we're going to live in. The bad thing about it is that it's too far away from home. It's on the other side of the city, close to where Ali works, so I don't really have a choice.

April 13, 1990

Ali and I have been married for two months now. His family is really nice and kind, except for his grandmother, who I can't stand. That woman is so bossy and controlling. She comes to our house and acts like it's her place. And she's always telling Ali that he should have never married me.

May 2, 1990

Guess what? I am pregnant. I just found out this morning. I can't believe this—I'm so happy! I haven't told Ali yet. I hope it's a girl, but I won't be disappointed if it's boy. I'm just glad I'm having a baby.

June 15, 1990

Guess what? It's a girl, and the due date is January15th! Ali's just as excited as I am. God, there's so much shopping I have to do before the baby is born.

August 22, 1990

I feel so fat and nasty looking; my stomach is huge. I'm only four months pregnant, but I look like nine months. I don't even go outside anymore, because when I do, I feel like all eyes are on me. So, I stay home and clean up and talk on the phone.

January 15, 1991

Today's my due date. Ali didn't go to work, because he says he doesn't want to miss anything. I told him there's nothing to miss, just go to work. But he says he wants to be the first to lay eyes on his first-born child.

January 16, 1991

Oh my god, she's so cute and adorable. She has light brown-goldish eyes. Her hair is dark brown, and her skin is so smooth. Her name is Aliyah Ali. Ali and I picked it out together.

February 12, 1991

This baby's driving me crazy! I can't even remember the last time I got any sleep. I don't even know what's wrong with her. God, I never thought taking care of a child would be this hard. She keeps throwing up everywhere, she has diarrhea, and she cries non-stop.

March 13, 1991

I can't do this anymore; the baby is getting on my nerves. It has been a month now, and she's still crying every single minute. What does she wants from me?!

June 3, 1991

Today I got a call from my cousin, the one who lives in America. She told me how she's trying to get us to come live in the U.S. with her, but I doubt it will happen. Many people try to help their families come to America, but it never happens. So, I'm not even going to bother to tell Ali. I don't want to get his hopes up.

August 5, 1991

My cousin Farah called again today. She says that she has everything worked out. and we'll be leaving next month for America, but I don't know if I should believe her. This is like a dream come true. I've heard lots of things about America, how they have good schools and better education. Ali thinks it's a great opportunity for Aliyah, and he thinks he can go back to school himself and become a lawyer.

September 12, 1991

Oh my god, we're leaving today. I'm happy and sad at the same time. I'm going to miss everybody here, and I'm going to miss living in Somalia. It's hard saying goodbye to everyone, especially Mom and Dad. We're taking an airplane. I've never flown in a plane before. I have to admit, I am kind of scared.

September 17, 1991

It's so beautiful here in America. We live in this big fancy white house in Miami. Turns out, Farah and her husband, Amir, are rich, and they don't have any kids, because they still think they're not ready. I find that a little odd. I've never met a couple that has been married for two years with no kids. Anyway, I have to go. Farah is taking Aliyah and me shopping.

* * * * *

This place is so different from Somalia. For one thing, the mall is enormous, and fancy. But what I notice is that the girls here pretty much don't wear any clothes. I mean their hair is showing, and they wear pants and little tiny tops.

January 15, 2004

Well, I haven't written in this journal for five years, and today is my daughter Aliyah's thirteenth birthday. She's the same age I was when I started this journal. In the last five years, I've been so busy as a mom. Guess what? I have two other kids, Jamal and Aisha. Jamal's six and in kindergarten, and Aisha's three. She's so pretty and charming. Ali is a great husband and father. He went back to school and became a lawyer.

You won't believe how big Aliyah has gotten. She's in seventh grade. She's one of the smartest students at her school. We're having a big party for her right now, and she has invited basically everybody from her school. I baked her a cake, her favorite. She blew out the candles and said, "Thanks, Mom."

I'm getting to know myself through my daughter.

Fifteen-year-old **Hana Mohamed** thought this book project was cool. "I like the fact that people outside Seattle or all across America would be reading our stories." Hana describes herself as kind, smart, and helpful, and she enjoys hanging out with friends and watching movies. She is inspired by her mother and plans to go to college and find a career she loves.

IF YOU DO HAVE
SOMEBODY TO TALK TO,
THEY'LL HELP YOU FIND
EVERYTHING, LET YOU
KNOW WHAT MATERIALS
YOU NEED TO BRING TO
CLASS, AND TELL YOU
WHEN CLASS ENDS.

How I Survived Changing Schools
Veronica Tinajero

Changing schools is not fun.

You don't know anybody, you have to learn the new school's rules, and you don't know where anything is. When you try to make new friends, you're not sure if they want to be friends with you or not. Some people could be racist or make fun of the way someone from your culture talks or act like they are better than you. They might also call you names for no reason.

(Still, you might discover that they're only acting this way towards you because they're jealous.)

If people at your new school don't like your style, they might tell everybody they know that you dress weird. They might say things like, "I buy my clothes at Nordstrom's. You buy your clothes at Goodwill, right?" They'll look you up and down and make faces at you.

People might not want to hang out with you if you're younger than them because they don't want others to think they're immature. If you're older than them, they might not want to hang out with you because they think you might boss them around when you hang out.

Not knowing anybody at a new school is not fun because you don't have anybody to talk to. If you do have somebody to talk to, they'll help you find everything, let you know what materials you need to bring to class, and tell you when class ends. If you don't have anybody to talk to, nobody will have your back if somebody wants to fight you, and everybody will think something is wrong with you when nobody has your back.

It's not fun not knowing where anything is at a new school because you might get lost. And your legs might get sore because you have to walk around trying to find things. It's boring because you could be doing something else, like hanging out with your friends.

Learning the rules at a new school can be difficult too. You have to remember if it's okay to wear hats, if kids in this school use lockers, or if it's okay to eat in class. And after you memorize all the rules, there's always a chance the school will change them and you'll have to learn them all over.

There are some good things about changing schools too. Your friends at your new school don't have to know about your old, bad friends. They don't have to know that your old friends got in trouble with the cops, skipped school, and were gang-bangers. And you don't have to see the people who didn't like you at the old school anymore, or hear rumors being spread about you.

Moving from school to school is very hard and not fun, but it gives you something to think about and remember, like saying goodbye to your friends, or regretting not saying goodbye to them. You might wish that you had let your friends know you were moving and changing schools.

But I also made new friends. I started talking to other people and becoming their friends, so I learned that sometimes making friends is very simple. Now I think that it will be easier to change schools again and deal with other changes that I have not dealt with before.

Twelve-year-old **Veronica Tinajero** is inspired by her two aunts. After graduating from college, she hopes to become a dancer, singer, model, or clothing designer. Until then, she expects to continue to enjoy playing basketball and hanging out. In fact, it's her basketball skills that Veronica likes most about herself.

"YOU LAY AROUND HERE
LIKE YOU ARE KING," HE
SAID IN HIS THICK IN-
DIAN ACCENT.
 I LAUGHED TO MYSELF
AND THOUGHT, I AM A
KING, AND IN FACT, I'M
KING OF MY WORLD.

King of My World
Schyler Mishra

I was out cold in my bed. The warm sunlight beamed through the blinds so I wrapped up in a blanket to keep the light out of my eyes. It was around 11:00 a.m. on a Saturday in October, 2006. Saturday is the only day I get to sleep in and relax before I go to work. Suddenly, I heard an obnoxious banging.

"Dammit," I thought. "It's my dad,"

The doorknob turned and the door swung open. My dad stomped in, nearly stepping on several pieces of clothes, and started complaining that I don't do enough around the house. I was only half awake and trying to figure out what was happening. Why was he in my room? I sat up in my bed.

"You lay around here like you are king," he said in his thick Indian accent.

I laughed to myself and thought, I am a king, and in fact, I'm king of my world.

He ranted some more and stormed out of my room. What the hell was he talking about? I lay back down and thought about everything that led up to this point—including why I moved to my dad's house in Seattle.

If you had told me fourteen months ago when I was living with my Mom in Everett all the things I would go through between then and now, I would have said, "What are you smoking? There's no way I'd ever do any of those things. Write two stories that were published in a book? Meet Bill Gates? Be on the front page of the *Seattle P.I.*? Go to graduate-level classes at the University of Washington? Get outstanding grades in all my classes, and have a job at Harborview Medical Center at the same time? That's impossible!" Before I moved in with my Dad, I lived my life carefree, without any regard to the future.

I was a senior and supposed to graduate from Cascade High School in Everett, but I goofed around in class, hung out with my friends, and completely screwed up everything. So much for my magnificent senior year.

I hadn't expected high school to turn out this way. I had seen all the high school movies and was excited about all the great things that were going to happen. Unfortunately life is not like the movies, and things don't work out like you expect them to.

When it came to school, my spirit had completely shattered. The only things important to me were my friends and having a good time. I cared about lunch, what was going on after school, and weekends. I just hung around school to see people, talk to girls, and to basically kill time during the day. Homework was last on my list of priorities. There weren't any glorious moments of me walking down the aisle to graduate, no senior trip, and no senior prom; I grew to scorn all of those events that I had at first anticipated.

It would be easy for me to make up excuses for why I screwed everything up as bad as I did, but I'm not looking for any sympathy from anyone. I hate the image of an "alternative student" that should get sympathy because he has problems. I am just a normal person who, due to a number of certain circumstances, ended up in the situation I am in now. I can blame the whole world for my failure, but it was my fault that things turned out the way they did. It wasn't that my parents didn't care, because they did. It wasn't that I was a victim of a school system that allows students to slip through the cracks. Parents and school played a small role, but the main person to blame was me. I know now I could have done the work then but my head was full of self-doubt. On the surface I seemed cocky and confident, but underneath I wasn't happy with my life and the direction it was going.

One day in particular stands out more than the others. It was another of the many scorching July afternoons in Everett, 90-plus degrees outside. The heat was becoming unbearable; every day seemed to drag on longer and longer. I'd just gotten out of the shower and walked into my room.

My friend Chris was sitting on my bed and staring intently at the TV.

"Hey your dad just called. He thought I was you and started yelling at me but I told him you were in the shower and you would call him back," he said without taking his eyes off the TV.

"Damn, really?"

"Yeah, he sounded pretty pissed off."

I didn't want to talk to my dad at all. I stood there as the fan blew a cool breeze on me thinking of all the possible reasons why he would call me. My dad believes that you must obey your parents at all times, no questions asked, like in India. But we don't live in India. Our last conversation hadn't ended well. I had told him that I didn't want to visit him anymore because we didn't get along. This wasn't what he wanted to hear.

"Fine. Don't come then!" he had said, and hung up on me.

Now he wanted to talk to me. I hesitated at first to pick up the phone; I dialed the number slowly and hung up right after it started to ring. After I had some time to think about what I was going to say, and how I was going to deal with whatever he had to say, I dialed again, expecting the worse.

Each ring seemed to last longer then the previous. I was hoping the answering machine would pick up. I thought I was home free and began to relax when I heard a click. "Hello?" I hesitated and said hello, and we began to talk. He wasn't angry. He seemed unusually relaxed and calm. He said I wasn't going anywhere in Everett and I should move in with him, so he could make me a "successful man." For some reason, deep in my mind I knew he was right, even though I didn't want to admit it at the time. I always did the opposite of what he said.

I paused for a few seconds, then nonchalantly told him I'd think about it and hung up. I didn't want to move to Seattle. It would be weird, especially with him, because he annoyed the hell out of me. I'd miss all my friends in Everett. I didn't want change. I didn't want to be in an unfamiliar city. But the truth was, I was getting bored with my situation. I knew something had to give eventually, and in the back of my mind, I knew I'd go through with it.

That summer would be the last time I spent hanging out with my friends in Everett. I knew that some kind of change was going to happen, whether I liked it or not. It was then I realized that many of the friendships I had weren't as strong as I believed.

When my dad came to pick me up at the end of August, I was very uneasy about what it was going to be like. I had packed up my clothes, my posters, and just about everything else that I thought I needed. When I was done packing, I looked at the walls of my room. They used to be covered in posters but now they were bare, covered in holes from the tacks.

I knew that this was the end of a chapter in my life. I had to say goodbye to my mom, which was very awkward. I had lived with her my whole life. This was the moment I'm sure she dreaded the most.

"My baby is all grown up. I can't believe you're moving out," she said.

"I know. I can't believe it either," I said with a smile.

We were both sad, but there was a feeling of hope and opportunity in the air. She knew I had to go in order to build a successful future for myself. I carried my stuff to the car and got in. My mom waved goodbye as we drove off.

When we got to my dad's house, I walked into my new room. I

looked around at the blank white walls and thought it had potential to look decent, once I got to work.

Two weeks later I started school at John Marshall. Let's just say it wasn't what I expected. At first, I was still messing around, not really caring too much about how I acted or doing the work the teachers assigned. Then a month later a speaker by the name of Skip Rowland came to our school. He was very tall and had broad shoulders. He was dressed slick but he had a very humble manner. He was from Project Mister, a class that teaches men of color about a number of important topics, including the importance of education, the economy, and how to succeed in a world fueled by global competition.

He said I needed to wake up and see how the world really worked. He said the school system wasn't designed for everyone. I thought I was rebelling against the system by not doing the work and messing around, but it was the exact opposite. I was working against myself. I woke up that day.

In Project Mister, I didn't slack off at all. I got there early and took notes every day. Most importantly I was actually interested in what we learned and excited to come to class every day. We were treated like college students; being late and not taking notes were not options in the class. Otherwise you were asked to leave and never return.

Everything began to change for the better. I got my grades up significantly. It was the first time I had ever done so well. Now I could lie in bed at night and not have all those negative thoughts about school in my head.

We went on field trips to places like City Hall, and the University of Washington, where I got the chance to sit in on Skip's classes. He taught in the School of Business. We went to Microsoft, where I asked Bill Gates a question in front of a live webcast. I chose a question that was on everyone's mind about whether Microsoft was going to develop an MP3 player to counteract Apple's iPod. The next day an article was written about me in the Seattle P-I because of that question.

I won an award from the Rotary Club and received scholarship nominations for my work. In 2006, I participated in the book project with 826 Seattle, which was my first experience writing a real story. I also got my first job that year.

With all these responsibilities hanging over my head, I couldn't flake out. I had to be held responsible. Maybe that's what I needed all along: responsibility. In just one year, I had completely changed every aspect of my life. I have a long way to go, but I have found my way to a path that will lead me to success. It's hard to believe so much can be accomplished in a year, but it shows the unpredictability of life—how fast your whole world can change.

Last night, my dad said, "I am the reason you are now successful man. Without me, you'd be nothing." I just looked at him and shook my head. My dad didn't play nearly the large part he thought he did. It was my blood, my sweat, and my tears that have made me successful. I can look myself in the mirror each day and honestly say, "I did it all on my own!"

"My ability to rise to the occasion," answers nineteen-year-old **Schyler Mishra**, when asked what he likes most about himself. He describes himself as outspoken, and lists working out, playing Xbox 360, and listening to music among his hobbies. His goal is to discover a career in college and then to like it, and he is inspired by "anyone who has become something from nothing."

CHANGE SUCKS. BUT
YOU CAN LEARN TO LIVE
WITH IT. JUST CRY YOUR
EYES OUT, BREATHE,
AND MOVE ON.

June: Worst Month in Existence
Shauna Lee

As soon as we started driving, I wanted to jump out of the van. I'd sprint back home and hide in one of my friends' houses until people stopped looking for me. There were problems with my plan, mostly just the fact that if I were to fling myself out of a vehicle at this speed I'd break my legs and wouldn't get very far before being recaptured. It played out well in my mind, though.

Rain splattered against the windshield while we stopped at a gas station. I kept my head bent over my book, enjoying how distracting it was. So far this had worked to drive away the stabbing loss I should have been feeling. The fact that I'd stayed up until three in the morning watching TV on the floor of my empty living room and was about to pass out from exhaustion might have had something to do with it, too. Either way I was glad for the numbness in my head.

After my uncle pumped and paid for gas and started the van again it only took us a few minutes to get out of town. I never realized just how small Ephrata was until I was leaving it. I think the population was a little bit above or below a couple thousand people and no one has ever heard of it. I know because every time I tell people where I moved to Seattle from I have to explain that it's over the mountains near Moses Lake.

I looked up a couple of times as we drove and most of the places I saw I'd been to at least once with either my friends or family. And every single memory was happy. I looked at my reflection in the rearview mirror, sure that some emotion would show on my face, but there was nothing. Completely expressionless.

Most of my friends lived in town. One up the street from me, a couple down the street, some across town. The friends I saw the most were the ones within walking distance. I remembered once when I'd walked up to…

Suddenly, a little bit of feeling seeped into my heart. Tears welled in my eyes and my heart raced. Right when the tears were about to come out I snapped my head up to glare at the ceiling. Luckily it worked and when I looked back in the mirror there was no sign that I'd almost cried. Good.

Yes, Mom had promised we would come back for visits so it wasn't like I would never ever come back again. But I didn't want visitation with the town I'd lived in for six years. I didn't want to maybe sometimes get to see my friends when I'd once been able to just walk up or down the street.

When my mother says, "Oh yeah, we'll visit," it really means "We'll visit when I have enough time off of work," or "when I have enough money for all the gas it'll take to get over there," or "when I have enough energy." Well, I wasn't going to be back anytime soon. It didn't really sit well with me that my sister got to spend the entire summer in Ephrata. It seemed a little unfair. She'd be with her best friend that she'd been practically living with all year while I went with Mom to help her unpack. What kind of a summer is that? Working all day long. It disgusted me. But my sister beat me to it, announcing her plans shortly after we found out we were moving. Even though it was a complete injustice, I'd just shut up, refrain from pouting, at least around my mother, and be a good girl. A helpful, smiling robot who's completely dead inside.

When my brain felt like it would overload from the book's small print, I looked out the window. We were finally out of town. A trailer, another trailer, a trailer so covered with rust that I had to wonder if that was just the paint, a five-year-old kid running with scissors outside a purple house from his cussing mother. I reopened my book. Well, I thought to myself. At least it's raining... I spoke too soon. Five minutes to be exact. Sunlight filtered through the clouds until they were gone, leaving clear blue sky. Most people love the sunshine and can't stand the rain, because it makes them sad. I am the complete opposite. Too much sunshine in any other time except for summer makes me depressed.

We parked at a rest stop after an hour on the road. The plans to escape reformed in my head only because I remembered one thing: school. I would be going to high school. In Seattle. With about a thousand other people. The hallways would be crammed, the school would probably be too big so I was guaranteed to get lost, and I'd be by myself until someone pitied me enough to say hi. Some enjoy talking and make friends easily. I won't utter one word around strangers unless someone else talks first. Which complicates things a little bit.

There were two possibilities I took into consideration while I drank the soda I got from the vending machine, completely ignoring the yells from Mom somewhere behind the van where she parked. (She locked the keys in the car.) Either I could hitchhike back to Ephrata or run. I discarded the first idea immediately when I imagined me—a barely five-foot tall teenage girl whose only means of defense is a pathetic routine of weak kicking and biting—standing by the side of the highway with my thumb out and a fake pleasant smile on my face for any psycho to easily claim. My second idea wouldn't work out much better. If I were to take off running down a highway, my mom wouldn't bother to chase me. No need. Knowing me, the farthest I'd get would be maybe two yards before accidentally straying into the way of a semi and being splattered over the asphalt in a bloody mess.

The odds were against me. For now.

"Ready to go?" I jumped when the driver's door slammed seconds later and my uncle started the engine. Apparently I'd underestimated how quickly they could rescue keys from a locked car. I held back my real answer, nodded (I think I might have uttered a "yeah") and we were off again.

I will spare you the details of the other three hours we were on the road because they were really, really boring. Tree after tree, a skiing place, more trees, a farm, a llama on a farm, still more trees. See? I'll just fast forward to when we pulled up behind our new home. That's right, I said behind.

A small blue rectangle in between another rectangle and a huge condominium across the street from a golf course. We had our own little parking place on the hill behind our house, since the neighbors took the only one in front. Red porch, white back door, a small shed that would barely even hold all of our boxes that we weren't going to bring in the house (mostly just stuff we hadn't been able to get rid of in time). On the outside the house looked like it had at least three bedrooms. I was warned ahead of time that it only had two but that it was "good-sized." I'd also been told this living arrangement was only until January. Both turned out to be wrong.

I soon found out that if you stand by the back door in the kitchen and turn all the way around you have an excellent view of the whole house. Two bedrooms side-by-side, one teeny bathroom, and a living room about the size of one bedroom (not counting the space with the front door and closet). If I were to guess I'd say this was the size of the back room and my mom's room of our other house combined. No, our old kitchen was as big as this place.

"This isn't so bad." Mom, finished talking with the landlord on the porch, walked in, looked around, and didn't show even a little sign of disappointment. She'd been assured by my father that this place was big enough for us and hadn't seen it until now. There were no pictures on the Internet. I swallowed the complaints and helped unload boxes instead. I thought: Just until January. Six months. Not that bad so shut up and look happy. It really wasn't so bad…but it would be better if…I said shut up!

Everyone left a couple of hours later when the living room and both bedrooms were crammed with boxes. The thought that I could have hidden in the van didn't hit me until I was lying on my practically bare mattress with nothing to do except watch movies on my small TV. I was miserable and completely alone. My sister was back in Ephrata, having fun with her friends and not alone at all. Meanwhile I was lying here under a blanket, miserable and bored out of my freaking mind. My sister got to have fun with her friends and I was here, suffering, wallowing in self-pity and anger at the unfairness of it all.

Eventually, when I thought I'd be driven insane from lack of human contact (besides Mom) I called one of my best friends from Ephrata, allowing myself to complain as much as I wanted. Long as Mom didn't hear. It would only make her feel worse about having to move. By the time I hung up, my head had cleared itself of numbness so nothing stopped me from crying anymore. I rolled over and bawled my eyes out until it finally got dark outside at about eight o'clock. I struggled to find someone to blame for this but grew even more frustrated when I couldn't think of anyone. The only one who had anything to do with this was my mom and I didn't have the heart to get mad at her. She got fired, couldn't find another job, wouldn't commute to other places where jobs were available, and ran out of money. If I were her and one of my daughter's fathers offered to help me find a house I'd take it in a heartbeat. Unfortunately, my sister's father didn't pull through, we didn't get the place in Shoreline because he didn't go look at it like he was supposed to, and we ended up here. Aha! I found someone! I don't know why but finding someone to direct all my anger at made me feel better. Good enough to fall asleep even though I had a splitting headache from crying and my eyes ached.

TAP. I heard…tapping. TAP. Wonder what that is. TAP. Getting a little annoying now. TAP. "Quiiit taaaapping!!" I yelled, my eyes still closed, halfway asleep. TAP. TAP. TAP. Okay now I'm gonna shoot someone. I leapt off my mattress, turning all the way around, but the noise wasn't coming from my room. Mom had left the door open when she came in to turn off my TV, so I immediately saw the water rolling down the window in the kitchen and the gray clouds blotting out the blue sky that was there yesterday. I tripped down the porch stairs, twisting my ankle but ignoring the pain. I stood on one leg, occasionally hopping to keep my balance, and stared up at the sky until I was practically blinded by raindrops. I really didn't care that I couldn't see, even when I was trying to get up the porch steps and nearly broke my ankle again, it really didn't matter. For the first time in about three months, since the day my sister and I came home to our mother asking our opinions on moving (a resounding, absolute no), I felt a little bit of happiness. Not complete euphoria, of course, rain doesn't have that big of an effect on me, but it helped a little bit.

The throbbing pain in my leg didn't hit me until I was sitting on my floor a couple of hours later after going to the store and eating breakfast. Now I had to unpack all my stuff, organize it, and try to refrain from just throwing everything at the walls. Pain was only one thing that contributed to my mood, which had turned bad again only a couple of minutes after I went outside. My resolution to act robotic, not to question or argue with commands, began to fail. My rebellious streak kicked in again no matter how desperately I tried to bury it.

I throw things when I'm mad. No screaming or crying. I go dead silent. And I don't throw things that easily shatter like glass. Just stuffed animals or pillows. But since I was trying to behave I avoided the boxes I knew had my stuffed animals in them. My plan was to just leave them in there, save unpacking those for another day when I wasn't so violent.

To further avoid violence I didn't get ice for my ankle. I let it throb so I wouldn't move around very much. I got a box I'd labeled "clothes" and cut it open with scissors instead of ripping it like I normally would.

Yep, this one was safe. Just all the clothes I'd put in without folding, not caring about the wrinkles. It'd all get washed anyway. It was calming to sit on the floor, folding my clothes and putting them in the dresser, nice and organized. And it surprised me that I remembered how to fold clothes. It's not the most difficult thing to do, it makes room in the dresser for more clothes, and it makes them look nicer. It didn't make any sense to me why I didn't do this back in Ephrata. Or ever in my life. Why did I always need to be so messy? How stupid.

My self-brainwashing was coming along nicely.

And then I saw it. The little red bear I'd gotten a couple of years ago on Valentine's Day. So small…soft….tossable. I just stared at it, arms hanging at my sides, wanting to close the box and forget about it. Then my head started: If he'd just gone to Shoreline and seen the freaking house we wouldn't be living in this freaking place. We'd have a nicer house, a better house, I'd have my own room. It's all his fault. It's all his fault. Blame him! Blame!

My arms shook to life, lifted the bear out of the box slowly.

Such a good year, I thought. It was such a good year before that. Remember when… I gritted my teeth and threw the bear against the wall without thinking, hearing the small thud it made before hitting the floor. A small fraction of rage faded away. I retrieved the bear and did it again. Another little bit gone.

And things are going to change. I'll go back and not recognize anyone. I'll be lost. Everyone will forget about me. Eventually they'll stop sending me messages, they'll forget me! I'll be completely alone. They won't love me anymore!

I accidentally let myself cry. It was completely untrue, I knew that, but right then it didn't sound so fake. I imagined when my friends would go to school. They'd think about me for a second then move on with their lives while I'd be here, dwelling on every last memory, starving for pity while they'd be perfectly content with my absence.

And after a couple of years they won't even remember me.

Looking back I'm appalled at myself for thinking that, even if it was only for a split second. Such a lie that it makes me sick now. But mental breakdowns aren't supposed to make sense. Even the really small ones.

I rolled over on the floor and cried. My heart actually started aching. For some reason I ran out of tears really fast so eventually I was just lying on the floor with my eyes shut, letting myself ignore the whole world and concentrate on doing nothing but wallowing in my own self-pity.

Poor me. Poor, pathetic me.

I opened my eyes and glared at the ugly brown carpet. I don't even have Internet, I thought. I don't have anything. And who in their right mind would pick this color for a carpet? It's hideous and I want to rip it out!

An hour passed. Then another one. Still hating life and the carpet. And fighting the urge to write all over those freakishly white walls.

Okay, this is really stupid. I sighed, annoyed with myself. I sat up and wiped my eyes, the anger and sadness fading away little by little, but never completely leaving. It's not that bad, I told myself. I'll go find the computer and put dial-up on it, even though it's going to be really slow. At least it'll be Internet. School is going to be horrible, that's completely unavoidable, but I can deal with it. And we only have to live here until January, then Mom will have saved up money for a new place. This isn't permanent. And even though I won't get to go back for visits very much, I'll still get to go. It's nowhere near enough but still, I'll live.

I finished putting my clothes away. Even though I really, really didn't want to live here and would give anything, including my arms and legs, to move back, the truth was I had no choice. Mom had offered to let me and my sister live in Ephrata, but there was no way that was going to happen. She's our mother and we'd been living with her for our entire lives, so there was no way we could possibly let her move without us. No matter how badly we didn't want to go.

At the end of the day, I sat on my mattress, watching the same movie over and over again, too lazy to get up and change it. Contentment replaced the negativity. Anger was still there; every now and then I'd think about either my sister's dad not going to Shoreline or the fact that I was here instead of Ephrata, The sadness hadn't completely gone away (still hasn't), but it wasn't as bad. It didn't completely consume me anymore.

I rolled over and before I fell asleep I remembered something that one of my friends who moved away a year ago told me. Moving isn't that bad. You get used to it after a while. Back when she told me, I didn't believe her. Moving from Ephrata would be the absolute worst thing that could ever happen, and I never, ever wanted it. But it's not that big of a deal anymore. I passed out into a dreamless sleep. She was right.

And now to bring my oh-so-tragic story to an end. Eight months have passed and I'm still living in the same microscopic house. "Hopefully we'll have found a place by June," is what my mom said, which really means, "Yeah, we're not going anywhere." So I'll more than likely be in Seattle for a while. Oh well. The hard part was leaving Ephrata. And now that's over.

I guess I should put some kind of a moral in here somewhere so here it is: Change sucks. But you can learn to live with it. Just cry your eyes out, breathe, and move on. That's what I did and so far I haven't died. I'm not completely miserable. I go to school, I'm friends with the greatest people in the freaking world, and I'm completely content with life. That doesn't mean there aren't things I wouldn't want to fix, changes I wouldn't want to make, but all in all, I'm perfectly fine.

Moving, having to start all over again after years and years invested in one place is one of those changes most people hate. It's horrible at first, especially if you don't have the Internet at home, but it gets better. Over time. Trust me.

Fourteen-year-old **Shauna Lee** figured
she'd have trouble writing for this book
project. "I thought it would be difficult,
since I'm so picky," she says, "but it
wasn't." Shauna enjoys surfing the Internet, writing, and reading. She finds her
inspiration from other writers and poets.
What is one of her goals? "To live."

I NEED TO GET SOME KIND
OF LIFE, THAT'S WHAT
MY BROTHER TOLD ME
ALL THE TIME WHEN I
TRIED TO GO WITH HIM IN
THE STREET.

The Day I Had Today
Daquan Bowens

The day I had yesterday was like the day before that. And the day before that. But today is a new day. I could tell that something was going to go right for a change because the stuff we hear in my hood from the time we get up in the morning is guns shooting and fights, man. You come in my hood and you bound to get in a gang or sell crack, weed, meth, or E, or get hooked on it and then get shot.
So when I don't hear nothing like that going on then I know that something good is going to go down and this would be the first time since… Since when? Since I was born. Maybe the day I'll have tomorrow won't be like the day I had today, and the day before that. Maybe tomorrow will be like no other day.

I need to get some kind of life, that's what my brother told me all the time when I tried to go with him in the street. We used to do a lot of stuff I knew we shouldn't be doing when I went with him, all weekend doing what the big boys did, but that was yesterday. Even when we were doing all that stuff he always had my back and he always told me that we needed to stop. He was the brother that I would always love no matter what.

My name is Ron and I have six brothers named Kalup, Dede, Clarens, CuQ, Chance, and Billy. My brothers and I all wanted the same thing in life. We all wanted to be out of the game, but we did not want to die trying to get out. To get out of the game we would have to die, and I am too sexy to die so that was not an option, not for me at least. There had to be some kind of alternative to that, but then I thought, do I really want out?

I think about my life and if the way I live is how I want it to be. How I always wanted it to be was with love and with money and that I go to get fitted with a red. Why? Because I bang, and you always got to rep your set, wear your colors, in or out the hood. You always got to have money, because you have no reason not to. They give you everything you need to make your money, for whatever you need it for.

That's how I got into all this. When my mom passed, some people came to tell me how to get money. I always got money from my mom before, but now I couldn't. I could see my brothers getting money and I always wanted what they had. They always got to go out. They got into a lot of trouble, and were in and out of jail, but they always came back. But then one day me and my brother got into an argument about whether we should stay in the gang or get out. He wanted to get out, but I wanted to stay.

I asked him, "Why would you want to betray us like that?"

He said, "You're betraying yourself. You could die any minute."

I asked him, "How could you come to that conclusion?" and then he walked out of the house. As I followed him outside, he got shot right in front of our house, right in front of me. I never even got to say I was sorry.

Do I want to get out? Do I want to stay in? I've got everything I want, but I'm not happy because I could die.

You could run, but that's like a sucker move to us. Nobody likes no suckers. If you run you're excluded from everybody's point of view. You can't be around me anymore because when I need you, you might run.

You could do a fight like the Four Brothers did and get out. You could get relatives and people you know and trust to help you fight. You can always get guns in the hood. But they always have more people on their side. It's like a war that you can't get out of.

You could go to a different gang. Most people, when they lose someone or something that means so much to them, they look for another alternative, and most alternatives are other gangs. Gangs are like family. They provide everything you need: money, love, everything.

My brothers and me need to get out. We want to get out. But look what we have: the money, the girls, the power. Why would I want to give that up? Maybe because I am not really happy and my mom always told me that money can't buy me happiness. I never did listen, but that was before she died on me. That's why I've got all these mixed feelings about whether I want to get out or not. What should I do? Should I give up the game or should I stay and gang bang, and maybe die because of it?

You tell me how I should end the story.

Who inspires fourteen-year-old
Daquan Bowens the most? He says
he just has to look in a mirror for the
answer. He also says he enjoyed working with 826 Seattle. One of his goals is
to make money, and he likes girls and
playing football.

I WILL NEVER PUT GUYS
BEFORE FRIENDS AGAIN,
BECAUSE IN THE END
YOUR FRIENDS WILL
ALWAYS BE THERE.

The Fact is I Still Love Him
Amanda Williams

I miss!
I miss your smile.
I miss your brown eyes.
I miss your voice.
I miss your hugs and kisses.
I miss spending time with you.
I miss being dorks together.
I miss your body lying next to mine.
I miss the love we made.
I miss the memories.
But most of all I miss you from your head to your toes.

I met Marc when I was fifteen. I was a freshman at Roosevelt High School, and he was a senior. I was dating somebody else at the time; his name was Tristan. It was lunchtime and I was with friends. Marc was with my friend James. James said hi to me. I looked over, and Marc and I both looked at each other. All I can remember from that day is his smile; he has a smile that lights up the whole room.

James knew Marc because they were family friends. I asked James all kinds of questions about Marc, but James just bad-mouthed Marc. I guess Marc was asking questions about me too, and James told him I had a boyfriend and wasn't interested. James did all of that because he liked me, too.

I started seeing Marc in the hallway, and he would always say hi and ask if I had my pet rat with me. A lot of kids had pet rats, and we would all bring them to school. After school one day Marc asked me for my number. I gave it to him, and he called later that night. We talked for hours about everything and anything. We started talking more, and he would hang out with me at lunch. Then Tristan just kind of left without saying anything to me. It was time for me to move on.

Marc and I were really good friends, and one day he asked me to come to his house. I made my friend Helena come with me. Marc had made his older brother light incense—I remember the incense burner on the floor. I thought it was so cute that he would do that. He lived with his older brother because his dad had passed away when he was younger. Marc took me by the hands and brought me into his room. His hands were sweaty, and he was so scared, and he said, "Amanda, will you go out with me?"

Of course I said yes. That day, February 7, 2004, changed my life. The next day he met my dad. I had never brought anybody home before. I know that Marc was scared. I could tell my dad really liked him. That made me so happy that he approved. Marc had dinner at our house, and they hit it off really well.

For our first date we went to the movies downtown, then back to his house, where he cooked me tortellini and chocolate chip cookies. I never had tortellini before, and my dad cooks a lot of Italian. I never had anybody cook for me before besides family. And I stayed the night at his house.

About three weeks later we were hanging out at my house, and Marc got a phone call. He went outside and started crying. I didn't know what to do. I asked him what was wrong, and he didn't tell me, so I went and got my dad. My dad gave him a hug, and they talked.

Marc came into my room and told me his mom died. I had no idea what to say or do, so I just hugged him. He told me that she was schizophrenic, and I kind of knew what that was, but I looked it up later on the computer. I was scared for him. He was really upset; he had planned for his mom and me to meet the next week.

After another three weeks, Marc got me a Chihuahua for an early birthday present. He knew I'd always wanted one. We went to North-gate Mall and I picked her out of three puppies. She was so little, she must have weighed two pounds at the most. Marc wanted me to name her Robin after his mom, but I felt really weird doing that. Later I was in my room watching "The Princess Diaries," and an ad came on the TV, and it showed Cinderella and Sleeping Beauty. That's when I decided to name her Princess, not just because of what was on TV, but because that's what my dad called me when I was little.

Meeting each other's families was a big step in our relationship. Marc and my family went camping in Friday Harbor. My family owns a cabin out there. It was the first time he met my whole family: my aunt, uncle, cousins, and my nana and papa. It's on the water, so we went swimming a lot and played with Princess. She was so little then, like eight weeks old. There are a lot of good memories from our time at the cabin. Marc was really quiet. I think he was overwhelmed with all the people that were there.

Thanksgiving was the first time I met his family, so I was nervous and scared to meet everybody, but they were all really nice. They asked me if was hungry, and I said no because I had just eaten at my house. Marc wanted me to try the sweet potatoes that his uncle Terry made, and he fed me with his spoon. His grandma and aunt saw, and smiled. I guess they thought it was cute. That kind of put me on the spot. All I was thinking the whole time was, "I hope they like me."

Marc's birthday is four days away from mine. I didn't know what to get for him. I wanted to know what he was going to get me (be-sides Princess) so I had my party a week early, but he didn't give me a present then. Instead he made it a four-day thing. He took me to the zoo one day. Another day we went to the Cheesecake Factory. I had never been there before. It was so funny: our waitress was named Amanda, and all the people sang to me. Then they brought out this cheesecake that had a sparkler candle in it. Marc thought it would be funny if he put the whipped cream in my hair. I got him back, though, and it was so much fun. When we were on our way back to his house, our hair smelled like vomit from the whipped cream.

The day before my birthday I asked my dad what we were doing, and he said nothing, so I was so bummed out. The day of my birthday Marc came to my house at eight in the morning with this giant Bundt cake. He'd carried it all the way over on the Metro bus. It had candles that didn't blow out, so there was candle wax all over the cake—it was so cute. It was the first cake he had ever made. Then we went to the movies. It was the best birthday I ever had.

For Marc's birthday we didn't do anything because his brother and friends took him out, but I got him a sweatshirt he really liked. By this time we had been dating about a year. I really loved him. My friends thought I was too young. I didn't hang out with them anymore.

I wanted to ask him to marry me. I was so scared. I had never even asked a guy out before, but I knew he was the one I wanted to share my life with. I made plans to ask him at Olive Garden, because he had never been there before. He couldn't make it because he wanted to hang out with friends. I was kind of pissed about that.

One day he showed up at the house, and I guess my friend told him what I was going to do so that kind of messed things up. I was so nervous, and so I asked him. He didn't say anything, but I know he thought it was cute. About a week later he was always playing "I Want To Marry You, Boy" by Paula Abdul, and he started introducing me as his fiancée, so I was happy.

We were inseparable. He was so much a part of my family. He and my dad really got along. They spent a lot of time together. When Marc wasn't with me my uncle Dale would always ask, "Where's your husband?" It made me feel good that my family liked him. Marc, my dad, and I would go see movies and go to the Cheesecake Factory and Game Works all the time.

Then Marc's brother, who had gone to college in Pullman, moved back in with him, and Marc started showing off and just getting really mean. Our relationship started going downhill. We started fighting about everything. One day I was over at Marc's house, and I was on the phone, and some girl started texting him. I was going through his texts, and there were like five texts from this girl. It said stuff like, "I miss you," "Do good on your test," and "I hope you feel better." Marc was sick, and he was getting ready to take the SAT. I was mad, so I got her number from his phone. Without saying anything to Marc, I left. I went home, called the number, and she answered.

I was just like, "Are you seeing anybody named Marc?"

She said, "No," and I told her his number. She said she didn't talk to anybody at that number.

I was being hella respectful. I wasn't just going to go off on her, because she probably didn't know about me. I said, "I have been seeing him for two years, and this is my man. I'm just trying to figure out what's going on." I was getting pissed off because she lied to my face, so I just got off the phone.

I hadn't talked to Marc for three days, and he called and asked me, "Why did you call my friend's girlfriend?"

I said, "Okay, well, why is she texting you?"

Marc said his friend used his phone, but his friend wasn't even at the house when I was there, and she wrote all that stuff that was related to Marc, so I thought he was lying. This kind of thing had never happened in our relationship before, though, so I gave him the benefit of the doubt. I have problems trusting guys. I'm not dumb. I know what really goes down. I live with all guys. It was hard for me to trust him. He thought because I didn't trust him, I didn't love him. But I did love him. I just feel that trust is earned.

It was hard for me to look at him the same after that. I was hurt by the whole situation. Later that day I got a phone call from my mom, and she was crying, and she told me that my great grandma had passed away, and I started crying. I got off the phone with her and called Marc, and I told him what had happened.

He said, "I'm sorry," and then he broke up with me. He was mad because I didn't trust him, but all the signs were there that he was cheating. We were broken up for three days. We had broken up five times before, and I was the one that always tried to resolve the problem and make it work. That was one of the things that I hated about

Marc: even if he messed up or he was wrong, I was always the one fixing the problems.

If things got too hard or emotional for him, he'd run away from the problem. He would bottle everything up and then just explode. It got to the point were he was saying mean things to me in front of his family, and I was still by his side through everything. I wanted him to get help or something, but I was getting sick of it.

I tried to make things work for months, but he stopped trying in the relationship, and it pissed me off. He had been planning on moving for weeks and one day I was at his house and he said something dumb like, "I'm going to change my number and not tell you where I move to."

I was like, "What?" Then he promised not to do that.

When I hadn't seen Marc for three weeks I went to his house, and we started fighting. He was acting really weird, and he said, "You can stay over tonight, but I'm moving tomorrow." I was pissed because he had never even told me. If I wouldn't have gone to his house I wouldn't have even known. He didn't want me to help because he thought I'd be in the way. Then he was just like, "I'm sorry we've been fighting so much," and he hugged me for like five minutes and said, "I love you." He was just acting funny. It made me feel like he was up to something, I just didn't know what. So I stayed over and left the next morning. Later I called him to see how things were going, and he said, "You can come up to the house when I get situated."

A month went by, and I hadn't seen him. We were still together, but when we talked we were always fighting. I'm the type of person that doesn't give up on someone I love. I fight till the end.

Around Easter Marc called and we fought. Then he broke up with me again! I could not believe he would do something like that. We had been together over two years, and he broke up with me over the phone. That hurt more than anything. I was never so hurt or angry in my whole life. I felt like he ripped my heart out. That day I not only lost a boyfriend, I lost my best friend. When my dad got home, I told him what happened, and he said, "You're still crying?" I felt as if I were all alone.

This past summer I was at my aunt's, and I started crying. She knew we had broken up, but she didn't know how or why. I told her what happened, and how for months I'd thought it was my fault. I thought I did something wrong. She told me that everyone needs a break sometimes, and if it was meant to be he'd come back. It's his loss. It still really hurt. I couldn't get over it.

I'm still not over it, and a year has passed, and I still think about him every day. If things had ended on good terms it would have been a lot easier on the both of us. We both said things and did things we didn't mean. I still miss him and love him very much. If I could tell him one last thing it would be that.

The main thing our relationship was lacking was trust. We tried to be adults too fast; we were still just kids. I'm a lot older now, and I know that I have to let more people in than I have. I tried to have a relationship with someone else mainly just to get Marc out of my head. If anything, it made me think of him more. We broke up because I still love Marc and always will.

I made a lot of mistakes last summer that I'm not proud of. If I could change anything it would be the way the relationship ended. That hurt more than he will ever know. One thing that did change is I will never put guys before friends again, because in the end your friends will always be there. I have also learned that when you care about someone you don't just walk away. I fought till the end. You never think you're going to find your soul mate at fifteen, but I did. He meant the world to me.

I hate!
I hate what you said.
I hate that you don't care.
I hate the fact you don't call.
I hate that I can't let go.
I hate the person you became.
I hate that you lied.
I hate the fact you didn't try.
I hate that you're not around.
I hate that I don't know you anymore.
I hate how you left.
I hate the fact I lost my best friend.
Most of all I hate that I don't hate you. I love you.

"My dad inspires me to keep moving and not give up on my dreams," says eighteen-year-old **Amanda Williams**. With that in mind, her goal is to move out of the house and start her own life. In the mean time, you can find Amanda playing basketball, hanging out with friends, and shopping. What did she think about this book project? "I'm very excited to accomplish this. Not many people can say they have written for a book before."

I LOVED LOOKING AT
THE MOUNTAINS WHEN
I RODE BY; THEY WERE
THE PRETTIEST PART OF
THE WHOLE TRIP. THEY
WERE AS BIG AS THE
MALL OF AMERICA AND
HAD LOTS OF PRETTY
COLORS, LIKE A RAIN-
BOW, LIKE ALL OF THE
COLORS FROM LIGHT
BROWN TO DARK BROWN
AND VERY LIGHT RED,
LIKE BLOOD ON THE
MOUNTAINS.

Why Do I Have To?
Amira Elhuraibi

Moving is so terrible that I would rather drink out of a dirty toilet than move again. You have to pack and throw away your belongings, and if you are like me, who traveled by Greyhound, you can't bring your pets along with you. You also have to leave behind your relatives.

I was born in Minnesota on August 14, 1995, the sixth child in a family of eight kids. I was a happy kid. I'm still a kid. When I was five years old, I was the second youngest child in the family. I got more toys than my three older brothers and two older sisters. My parents bought me Barbies and roller skates, even when it wasn't a special occasion. My brothers and sisters, on the other hand, only got clothes, and grown-up stuff, like shoes. Those years went by so fast.

When I was ten I found out we had to move to Seattle. My mom and stepdad wanted to get out of Minnesota because the crime got bad and my mom and little brother almost got shot on the city bus. They were sitting in the bus and a bullet went through the window over their heads. At first I thought moving would be okay, but then my mom said that we had to leave most of our belongings behind because you cannot have a heavy load, so I was mad about that because I liked most of my stuff. I had it for a long time. They were my favorite things. Also I would miss my dad very much.

And we had to leave our dog, too, and her puppies. Her name was Spliff and I loved her so much because she loved me. She had her babies on Halloween. When we went to go trick-or-treating, she'd had another one by the time we came back. That's why I was really mad; I didn't want to leave them. So that's why I hate moving to new places, and because I have to go to lots of different schools.

My stepdad came to Seattle first because he wanted to get everything ready for us. He said we should move here because there is a lot less crime, and also because he had a brother and lots of friends in Seattle.

Me, my mom, my older sister, and my two siblings moved to Seattle on the Greyhound. My older brothers and one older sister stayed in Minnesota, which made me very sad. When we went on the Greyhound, it was ugly, stinky, and full of old smelly people, and the bathroom had pee on the floor. The people smelled like cigarettes and old perfume and cologne. I had to sit by this old lady who stunk like rotten cheese, and she was as fat as a door. I had to use the nasty, smelly bathroom with nasty chewed gum on the wall. The bus had poop on the floor and food everywhere. I always had to switch seats because new people would always get on the bus. At nighttime the people in the back of the bus would be drunk, and since they were drunk they were really loud, and I could not sleep. It was a very long trip, two days long, and I hated those two days.

I kind of liked it a little when it was morning because I knew that was one less day on the nasty bus. I loved looking at the mountains when I rode by; they were the prettiest part of the whole trip. They were as big as the Mall of America and had lots of pretty colors, like a rainbow, like all of the colors from light brown to dark brown and very light red, like blood on the mountains. When I would go by them I was so fascinated that when some smelly person sat next to me I did not care. When we arrived in Seattle it was not cool because there were lots of homeless people outside of the Greyhound station. They smelled like the pee on the bathroom floor of the bus. It was raining, and I hated it because it was really cold and I got wet. When I got off the bus I put a tag that was on my stuff on me and said to ship me back to Minnesota, but my stepdad was there to pick us up. He got to the bus station before us so he was not late.

When we first arrived we went to eat at the free place in Seattle where people with no money and no place to stay go. We went to the mission, and they helped us stay in a motel the first night. The next day we went to go see downtown. I thought it was gross because it smelled like pee. We went to the store to buy something to eat. The next night we stayed at another motel. I kept thinking, why do I have to move into all these motels and move the next day?

We are now staying at the Wallingford Inn. We have been there for a long time, like six months. That six months I was wondering where my dad was, and then he called. He had moved to Tennessee. I was so glad I found out where my dad was.

Then the INS took my stepdad away because of an overdue visa. When the immigration took him my mom was, and still is, sad. My mom goes to visit him every week at the Tacoma immigration jail. And my family and I went to court; we hope he will get out soon, like in two months.

My mom enrolled us at John Marshall Alternative School. Two days later I went to the school and I really did not want to meet new friends because we were going to move to a new place. I made a new friend but she left. I made another new friend. Her name was Monica, and she was shy at first, then she started to be my friend.

And now I kind of like it here. I still miss Minnesota. The weather in Washington is not like the weather in Minnesota. The weather in Minnesota is much colder with a lot of snow. In Washington, the winter is not that cold, but I do not know about the summer yet. In Minnesota the summers are really hot. I don't like the weather in Washington. I miss the snow.

The thing that changed my mind is the way the people are here in Seattle. They are mostly like the people in Minnesota. They are nice to each other, and the way it is in the schools it's much easier than in Minnesota to get along with everyone. I am used to living here in Seattle; also there are not as many changes now. We're moving into a townhouse community soon. My stepdad is still in the immigration jail. Now the rest of my family wants to move here, like my grandmother, and my aunties, and my older cousins. I miss them so much. I hope they move here.

Who inspires eleven-year-old **Amira Elhuraibi**? Her father and her mother, she says, "because if there is a problem my mother makes it easier for the family." Amira plans on becoming a doctor. She liked this book project for the publishing and educational opportunities it gave her and her classmates.

THESE MENTAL SCARS
WILL NEVER GO AWAY.

My Special Curse
David Ryan Richter

My name is Xiu. I grew up on the planet Tatooine. Always sandy,
always hot. There was never anything to do there, only drugs. Mother
and Father had troubles with the Hutts all of the time; they usually
owed the Hutts money for drugs or bets on the races.

Me, I never got along with the other children. They would say I was
weird; they would throw rocks at me. I fought back every time. That
was how I was taught; never let anyone step on your toes, fight back
so they won't do it again. This would lead to trouble with parents and
teachers.

When I turned fourteen I knew I wasn't like everyone else. My
mother always told me that I was "special," that what I had was a
blessing but at the same time a curse, that whoever got to know me

would forever be a different person. I am a leader; people look up to me. Kind, caring, loving, gentle. Everyday, no matter what, I could always make anyone smile or laugh, even my enemies.

Then the curse: I seem to be a happy person, but really I am far from that. My emotions are of a higher magnitude than others'. Anger is the worst. When I feel anger my whole body is consumed with hate. Images of passionate violence run through my mind—nightmares, if you will. Ultimately, I care too much about little things and overlook the important subjects, and even my best friends tend to grow distant from me.

My mother: fourteen years of drugs and alcohol. After all the hell she went through she was finally sober and had found serenity. My father: oblivious. In his mind, he doesn't have a problem and yet every day, there are the drugs, pain, depression. Lost in a world of hate, he blames everything on everybody else. Every time I see him I have to listen to the lies. But are they really lies? What if he is right? If he is, I would have a whole new perspective on everything that I've dealt with, all the hell, the fighting, the yelling, pushing, and drugs. I hated it. I still hate it. These mental scars will never go away.

Imagine. Five years of age, my mother's and fathers friend's are over. I hear the yelling. This time there was concern in my father's voice. "What the hell are you doing? Get the blaster away from your damn head! It's not worth it, you have kids to take care of!" Although I was young, I knew what that meant. Fear struck. My mother's friend Tamma took me outside and tried to comfort me. Still, a tremendous amount of fear and adrenaline flowed through my body. I tried to see what was happening, I was restrained. Tears streamed down my face and I was growing weak from trying to pull away from the adults. I heard the sound of a blaster go off, then sparks. Everyone rushed into the house and saw that, luckily, the blaster shot had gone through the window. Mother was out cold, and Father was in shock. At first he thought she was dead. From then on, I was afraid of my parents' fights, and worried that maybe they might die from the drugs.

Drugs—nothing but pure evil and hatred. Lies. Seven years of deception. I couldn't take it anymore, and then the day came … December 25. Life Day, meant for happiness and joy, until I knew

that he wasn't coming home. I was at my grandparents' house celebrating Life Day with presents, drinks, and food. My grandfather
was fed up. He said, "You're not ever going to see your father again."
I exploded with vulgar expressions. Next time I saw my father he was
on Dethstix. Fidgeting and jumpy, very paranoid, he was accusing
my grandfather of things I had never heard of before. I was finished, I
had given up. I told myself, "I'm gone—away from all the bullshit."

I moved in with my mother. She was happy. We moved from Tatooine to Dantooine. I still thought about my father. Is he still alive?
Where is he? Will he ever come back? Every day I thought about this,
and hoped that someday he might come and see me or give me a message. Nothing. Again, I waited for nothing.

"Xiu, Don't worry about your father. He does what he does and
maybe someday he'll find the light and won't be stuck in a hole."

I said nothing, but depression took over. I left, on my own.

If you find fifteen-year-old **David Ryan Richter** daydreaming, don't worry: it's just one of his hobbies. His grandfather inspires him, and his goal is to become a great artist and live a happy, stress-free life. What did he think of this book project? "Fun!"

MY MOM IS MY BEST
FRIEND.

The Life of a Metaphorical Mood Ring
Jami Ram

This is my life. These are my hardships. These are my rises and falls. These are my changes. This is who I am.

I would have already had a novel written if I said how many house moves we have had. Moving all the time hasn't been the easiest but when you've done it all your life you get used to it. It always seems like just when I get comfortable, we leave.

My father hasn't always been exactly there for me. When I was younger I almost never saw him.

About four months ago my mom and I were unpacking our new house. We were going through all my old baby stuff and there was this tape that had my dad and me together when I lived in Bonny Lake. My parents' friends were playing with me and I was really comfortable with them. When one of them asked me if I wanted to go to my father, I looked at my father like a stranger. You could tell I didn't want to, but when they asked me if I wanted down I was all peppy and said yes.

My mom had me when she was fifteen and thought my father would be her love forever. Nope. She soon realized when she was pregnant that my father wasn't a man up to his responsibilities. Since then she has pretty much been on her own. She's been through a lot, and I went through it with her. My mom is my best friend.

When I was three my mom met a man, let's call him J.G., whom she thought might be her husband and life partner. They were together a year and then they had my sister Ash. Since my dad was never around, J.G. treated me like I was also his daughter and I liked him too. They were engaged for a year and then he took her car and committed a crime. He ended up in jail for a year. This was a wake-up call for my mom. She was on her own again.

When I was six she met a man who would actually become her husband. I personally never really cared for him but they had my sister Laina and I learned to put up with him. I guess I figured I had to since he was my stepdad.

When I was seven my father told me I had a sister named Kayla. She was six and we were going to meet her. My sister and I clicked instantly! While my father and her mom discussed legal matters about my sister, she and I played. By the end of the night we were best friends but we had to leave. We tried to play like we were glued together but it didn't work. It was years until I met her again.

When I was nine I moved into my grandma's house in Roseburg, Oregon, for the school year. This was a big change for me considering I almost never lived anywhere without my mom.

The following summer I moved back with my mom to Tacoma. Everything was fine until June and my stepdad started messing up. He ended up in prison.

My mom, my sisters, and I moved to Pass Christian, Mississippi, to live with my grandma Laura and her husband. At first I was excited, then I became scared when I got there. I didn't really like the heat. Even at night it was blazing. We lived there a few months, then my grandma and her husband had a falling out so we moved back to Washington.

My mom wasn't really able to take care of my sister Ash and me without my stepdad so she moved to her in-laws' house and my sister Ash and I moved into her dad's parents' house. My mom and stepdad ended up back together when he was released after a year in prison. Ash and I moved back in with them.

When I was eleven Grandma separated from her husband and came to Washington from Oregon. She lived with my auntie Trae for a while but then when I was twelve she wanted to stay with us after my auntie couldn't tolerate her anymore. Unfortunately, my grandma has a way of getting under people's skin. She will ask question after question and after the twelfth question you start to get irritable. My grandma has this intolerable need to know everything.

Not considering this problem my mom convinced my stepdad to let her stay with us if we rented a house in Tacoma. Because the house had a HUGE garage he accepted. Since we had my grandma's help with paying, my stepdad could afford to go to school and become a mechanic. Sadly my grandma moved out and we lost her house payments so my stepdad started working on people's cars when he wasn't at school. We met this lady Cryst and she moved in. Her sons stayed with us also on a part-time basis. My stepdad became associated with Cryst's children's father and agreed to fix his car.

Now every summer my grandpa arranges a camping trip at his private property by Canada, and for three days or so we hang out and have fun. My mom wanted the whole family to go, but my stepdad was swamped in work and had to stay behind. Instead, Cryst and her two boys came along. When we came back from camping, my stepdad was different. Little by little he started to change more and more. We suspected drugs.

In August, on my mom's birthday, he didn't come home. Next thing I know he tells me that he never had loved me at all. My heart broke in half. I felt worthless, I felt betrayed. I had to put those feelings to the side to step up as an adult along with my mother to console and nurture my family and what was left of my home. My mom and I discussed and decided that it was better that Ash move to her grandparent's house.

Ash moving away definitely hasn't been the easiest thing. It's pretty hard without her here with me since we grew up with each other our whole lives. It has been a big change for me and I'm assuming for her as well.

Soon after Ash left we lost our house so we moved in with these people we've known for about five years named B.A and A.J. It started off well enough but things started getting chaotic and under all the pressure my mom wasn't exactly coping. My mother, my sister, and I became stir crazy in this apartment. My whole attitude changed, everything about me did. I stopped attending school, stopped caring about life.

The summer of 2005 we moved again. My auntie Trae had moved in with her new boyfriend and let us rent out her condo in the South Seattle Skyway area. I couldn't really say that I liked this move. I didn't know anyone but I was willing to give it a chance. One of the first things we did after settling in was go and enroll me in Dimmit Middle School, a predominately African-American and Asian-American school.

My mother has always said that color isn't something you see on people, you can only see who their person is on the inside and judge by that. Living in Tacoma the majority of my whole life kind of revolved around those rules. At first it was okay at the school but then this boy J.J. who was black and Mexican started liking me and I liked him too. That's when the problems started. This other mixed girl started harassing me and got all her friends to join in. One day when there wasn't a supervisor in the P.E. locker room she and her friends attempted to jump me. One girl got suspended but the girl that started it all didn't have anything happen to her. This just made me more introverted. Less and less I went to school until finally I stopped all together. In about April 2006 my mom sent me to live with my dad to finish the school year.

At the end of June I moved back with my mom. Now I'm going to kind of "rewind." In August 2005 my mom met a man named Deaundre. At first I didn't really care for him but then I got used to him. I honestly thought he might be around for a good portion of my life but it got rocky. He started being crazy and in July 2006 my mom tried to break up with him. The next day they split up and Deaundre showed up at our house, very angry. Luckily the night before my mom had picked up J.C. (a mutual associate between her and Deaundre) and he stood in like a bodyguard. My mom and J.C. ended up dating and are currently in a relationship.

In August 2006 my auntie lost her condo and we had to move out. We ended up in Parkland with my mom's really old friend Annie. At first it was okay but Annie started problems between my mom and my mom's boyfriend. Little by little J.C. started to change. I think he went stir crazy in Annie's house. He explained that just the presence of her and her house made him feel crazy and angry. It reminded me of the movie Amityville Horror.

One day Annie decided that J.C. didn't need to live there anymore. He went to this house in Hilltop but he would never call it home. My mom didn't have anywhere to go at the moment because she had us kids to think about so he was stuck out there. Annie started pushing my mom to move out. My mom was finished so we moved into my grandma's studio apartment on Fremont Avenue and stayed there. J.C. still lived in Hilltop though so my mom would go pick him up and drop him off.

One day when my mom and him were driving him back to Hilltop they had an argument. As they were making up he told her he loved her and then she got pulled over. The cop said he had a warrant for J.C.'s arrest. The verdict being he was to serve time until November 2006. But in November, they said he hadn't served his past D.O.C time (which he actually did serve in an earlier year) and said he won't be released until November 2007. We ended up moving in with my grandma in Lake City.

At first it was just my sister, my grandma, my mom, and my great uncle Rich's roommate. In January I got in contact with my dad's sister, my auntie Andy. She came to visit us and decided to stay. Now she and part of the time her sons stay with us. It's kind of hard having her sons there because they are two and three so they are very rambunctious and very jealous of each other. I would have my own room but we all share it: Andy, her boys, and me.

Moving to North Seattle I met this guy; he and me dated a bit but this boy's whole views are very different to me. My whole attitude changed though. Somehow he made me a happier person. But I'm not giving him full credit; I think the move helped also. I go to school and finally this is a change I'm happy about. My mom has a great job and is starting as a silent partner in her new maid business now. Soon she will go back to college to get a degree in massage therapy. Life is great!

Before I always thought my changes were for the worse but if they hadn't been made then I wouldn't be here and who I am today.

Fifteen-year-old **Jami Ram** doesn't believe in making extensive plans for the future, though she plans to graduate from high school. She prefers, instead, to live life to the fullest and experience as many "positive things as possible." Jami's hobbies are writing, poetry, eating, sleeping, coloring books, and MySpace.

IT WAS LIKE A SCRAPE
THAT YOU GET WHEN
YOU FALL: JUST PUT A
BAND-AID ON AND LET
IT GET BETTER, BUT NO
MATTER WHAT YOU WILL
ALWAYS HAVE A SCAR.

The Big Move
Heather Hoyt

Ripped Away

Moving to Seattle tore Emma Lee from the life she knew for seventeen years. It ripped her from everything she loved back in Silverdale: photography, music, shows, and friends. She lost them all with the move.

The Rocky Horror Picture Show was one of Emma Lee's favorite movies. The first show she ever saw was on Friday the thirteenth. The Rocky Horror Picture Show is an audience participation show. It was the best. You could do just about anything; you could cuss, scream, or whatever you wanted. She'd go with her friends Andrew, Amber, and Andrew's mom. Emma Lee loved The Rocky Horror Picture Show so much that she'd planned to work at the theater, being part of the crew that got to set up the stage and work on sound, costumes, lighting, and props. But then she had to move two days before her job there started.

Her Silverdale friends consisted of people she'd known for four years to those she'd known from kindergarten. They were pretty much her life. She had a few best friends: Amber, Andrew, Tony, and Christina. The five of them would always be at the mall hanging out with their "Mallrat" friends. Amber and Emma Lee were inseparable, and sometimes Andrew and Emma Lee were, too; he and Emma Lee always hung out, went to the mall, The Rocky Horror Picture Show, and to movies like Four Eyed Monster. There were other Silverdale kids who became best friends, too. She met Shawn, Jack, Samantha, Travis, and many other people.

Moving to Seattle was lonely for Emma Lee. The Internet came into her life and helped her stay in touch with a lot of her friends. Emma Lee spent a lot of time online. She was always on MySpace, Yahoo, AIM, and MSN talking to her friends.

Tired of Hiding It From the World

Emma Lee had another problem, as well. It was a problem with her uncle, and it had been happening since she was five. It stopped when she was fifteen and had a boyfriend. It was a problem she didn't talk about for a long, long time. When she did, when she finally worked up the courage to talk about it, no one wanted to believe her. In fact, everybody turned on her, even some of her friends, and her whole life was messed up.

Emma Lee lost everything she knew and loved.

A Big Spiraling Pit of Darkness

That's when it all pretty much fell apart, and Emma Lee's life went into a big spiraling pit of darkness. It sucked to lose everything she knew; she got lost, especially because she didn't want to move. Her life got screwed up because of her uncle. Emma Lee just wished he hadn't done that stuff to her, because she would still have had the life she grew up with.

She became suicidal. She did drugs, smoked pot, popped pills, railed pills, ODed on pills, and always drank, and always cut her wrist. She thought those things would take away all the issues and all the pain. But it didn't, and she realized drugs and alcohol would not solve the problem. It might take the pain away for a little while, but it didn't take it away one hundred percent, and didn't erase what happened. It was like a scrape that you get when you fall: just put a Band-aid on and let it get better, but no matter what you will always have a scar.

When she was sober, she would do things like lock herself in her bedroom and turn up the music, drowning everything else out, or she'd do photography. Photography let her express her feelings when she was upset.

Things to Live For

A lot of changes occurred after Emma Lee moved to Seattle. Life was getting better, but some things never changed. There were a lot of ups and downs. This sucked for Emma Lee, because she was afraid of being suicidal again, but she knew she had things to live for like her mom, her siblings, her family, and her best friend Amber, who all were on her side when she told her secret. They all helped her through so much.

Emma Lee has lost touch with a lot of her old friends and half of them aren't even her friends anymore. Andrew and Emma Lee no longer talk. Travis and Emma Lee have had a distant relationship.

Emma Lee hasn't been to any shows in Seattle. She kind of gave up on that because she is no longer friends with Andrew. So she just listens to music on the radio or on CDs. It's some sort of way to vent. But she feels that someday soon, in a year or less probably, she will return to shows, and mosh it up in the pits like she used to. Hopefully.

Emma Lee doesn't go to The Rocky Horror Picture Show anymore, either. She feels like if she went in Seattle, she wouldn't enjoy it because her best friend Amber wouldn't be there to enjoy it with her. Emma Lee thinks it just wouldn't be the same. But as soon as she can she will return to Silverdale for another show.

In six months, when Emma Lee turns eighteen, she's going to move back to Silverdale and go back to school there until she graduates from high school, and then go to college to get into photography. She still picks up the camera and enjoys taking photos. It's become a daily thing for Emma Lee. She takes pictures of her family and friends.

She has made some interesting friends at her new school in Seattle. At first she was distant from them, but the more she hung out with them, the closer they became. She is kind of glad she moved to Seattle, so she can see what other places are like.

Life has been getting better for Emma Lee, sort of. Her family has had a rough time and is now coming through it. Her mother has a new job and her career is taking off. Her brother has shared the moving experience with Emma Lee and she is grateful to him for it. Emma Lee just hopes that someday her uncle will have to face the consequences for what he's done.

These are the changes Emma Lee had to deal with for twelve years of her life.

Afterword

These days Emma Lee is getting better. She is in counseling. While she has complicated depression and horrible panic attacks, she is now getting help. Emma Lee is wishing and hoping life will get better within the next year or so.

"I am inspired by small things and most of the time huge things," says seventeen-year-old **Heather Hoyt**. The list of huge things includes her friends, especially her best friend, Megan. Heather's hobbies are writing and photography, which makes sense since she plans on becoming a photographer and writer.

I WASN'T ASHAMED OF
MYSELF, BY ANY MEANS.
I HAD JUST BECOME
ABNORMALLY AWARE
OF HOW COLD-HEARTED
PEOPLE WERE.

My Life As a Statistic
Kathy Graves

About 750,000 teenagers become pregnant each year. Of them, only 250,000 will go on to complete high school. From there, only 3,750 teenage moms will go on to college.

My name is Kathy, and I am one of those 3,750. I am a statistic.

I started running with the wrong crowd at an early age. I saw things no child should have to see. I experimented with several different drugs before I even made it to eighth grade. When I got older, I found myself in dangerous situations in which I was lucky to have survived. Waking up in an unfamiliar living room with my head pounding from the previous night's worth of drinking and drug use had become habitual for me when I was twelve. My mom suspected marijuana, but I did a good job hiding all the true damage I was doing to myself. I preferred the hard drugs.

My father was never really around when I was growing up. He was homeless in Seattle for most of my youth, due to his life-long battle with alcoholism. I grew up in Selah, a small town in eastern Washington. Downtown Selah never had homeless people, like downtown Seattle; I never had to deal with looking into the eyes of a homeless man with no money for food and picturing my father's face. So even though I knew that my dad was homeless while I was growing up, the reality of homelessness never really hit me until I was a teen.

Around the time I was thirteen, my mother and I started fighting more. We were both stubborn and as a result I was told on several occasions she didn't want me in her home. Most of the time I didn't want to be there anyway, so I started couch surfing. I would spend one night here and one night there, never really knowing where I would go next or whether or not I'd be fed.

My mother started calling me in as a runaway. The police would find me and take me to Crisis Rehabilitation Center (CRC), where I would stay for three days until my mother would get me out, and the cycle would continue. I didn't feel welcome at my mother's house anymore. Sometimes I would call the cops on myself so I would be guaranteed a place to sleep and food to eat.

During one of my stays at CRC, my mother filed an At-Risk-Youth Petition. From then on, the police would pick me up and take me to juvenile hall. This went on from October of 2002 until April of 2003. During that time, my father had admitted himself into an inpatient program. When he completed the program and got his own place, he came and got me. I moved to Seattle with my father. My mother had been talking about moving to Alaska and it would be years before I would hear from her again.

Things were good for a while at my father's house. Then they started to go downhill. I was running the streets and would stay gone for as long as I pleased and my father had started drinking again. By the time things finally boiled over my father found himself back in treatment, and three months after turning fifteen, I found myself facing my ultimate metamorphosis.

I was a freshman in high school when I found out I was pregnant.

I was living in a group home for girls, which ironically specialized in aiding teen mothers. Since my father was in his intensive inpatient program and my mother was M.I.A., I was able to skip the dreaded "telling the parents" part for a while. I was almost five months along when I finally told my father. By the time I was able to locate my mother and let her know, I had already been a parent for three months.

My new school was Auburn High, located in the upper-middle-class area of Auburn, a smaller city south of Seattle. Not only was I way out of my comfort zone of Seattle, but I was attending an enormous school full of people I didn't know—people who grew up together, people who went to all the same schools prior, people who were nothing like me at all. It was hell.

I had horrible morning sickness. I remember the embarrassment I felt having to explain to my first period science teacher that I may have to run out of class occasionally due to my pregnancy and the inability to keep anything down. I remember the looks I would get from my fellow classmates as I ran out of class, the times I cried in the girls room because I was too scared to go back to class, and the times I wouldn't go to school at all just to avoid the hassle.

My classmates all treated me like I was really different from them. No one would talk to me, only about me, in whispers to their friends. I felt branded, like I walked around with a big sign saying, "I Am Pregnant!"

It wasn't just the students who embarrassed me either. My health teacher would regularly ask me questions in the middle of class about pregnancy while we were studying the human reproductive system, causing a tidal wave of stares and snickers. I remained at that school for three months. Three months of whispers, three months of eating lunch by myself, and three months of being used as an example in my health class. I wasn't ashamed of myself, by any means. I had just become abnormally aware of how cold-hearted people were.

During my stay at the group home I would make a six-hour round trip, courtesy of King County Metro, every Sunday. First, I would visit my father in rehab. On one of those visits, I told my father the news. I was so scared. During the entire three hours on the bus head-ing to see him, I had prepared what I was going to say.

When I finally arrived, I asked him if there was a place we could talk privately. He directed me to a small room in a remote part of the facility. We entered the room and both took a seat. I opened my mouth preparing to blurt out my speech I had so painstakingly organized. Instead, my throat went dry and I couldn't speak. We sat there in silence. After what felt like an eternity all I could say was, "I am pregnant."

We sat there, in silence once more, and tears began to well in his eyes. I thought about how he must be so disappointed in me. I had let him down. I also started to cry. After what felt like yet another eternity, he finally spoke.

"Congratulations."

The conversation started to flow. He told me he wanted me to keep the child. I reassured him that not only had I already come to that decision but I was nearing five months, so in reality I had no choice. We talked about when I found out and why I had waited to tell him. We talked about my boyfriend, Mike, and about what to expect in the future. My dad told me I shouldn't be surprised if Mike didn't stick around and I told him not to be surprised if Mike did. We talked about moving back in with each other as soon as he had completed his program.

My father found us a house and my brother, Jon, and I moved in. Shortly after, my dad took me to get enrolled back into the Seattle School District. I wanted to go to John Marshall because I had heard through the grapevine that Marshall had a daycare available for the students.

My first day at Marshall was intimidating. I prayed that it would be nothing like Auburn High, and it wasn't. I found that not only did they have an on-site daycare available for the students, but a class for teen parents. The teacher for the parenting program, Audra Gallegos, was extremely friendly and welcoming, which made the transition into the new school a lot easier. The atmosphere was so much more understanding then Auburn High. I was relieved. As freshman year ended and summer approached, my belly began to show more. I finished my freshman year of high school six months pregnant.

That summer was difficult for me. My father went to jail and my brother had been staying at his friend's house. At fifteen and pregnant, I was left living alone in my father's house. My boyfriend bought me food and made sure I had things I needed. I tried applying for benefits, such as food stamps, but I was denied. Every agency I went to blindly turned me away. I even spoke with Child Protective Services looking for some help and still received nothing. I felt helpless, lost in a cycle of systems created to help everyone, it seemed, but me.

I had never had to worry about things like this before. I was too young to have had to. With nowhere else to go, I moved in with my dad's ex-girlfriend. I stayed there for the remainder of my summer until my dad got out of jail. Then I moved back in with him.

I began my sophomore year almost ready to pop. I was nine months pregnant. Three weeks shy of my due date, my stomach was enormous! I had gained nearly seventy pounds and had been asked on many occasions if I was carrying twins. But no, there weren't two babies inside me—just one very big little girl.

As I waddled to and from my classes, I knew that I definitely stuck out. I only stayed at school for two weeks before I went on maternity leave. Pregnant students are given up to seven weeks maternity leave at Marshall. During that time, a teacher comes to visit you once a week to go over homework and different assignments, as well as collect any work that needed to be turned in. At first, maternity leave was kind of boring. All I did was play video games and watch movies with my dad. I couldn't really go anywhere, or do anything. All I could do was wait.

I was on maternity leave for only a week when on Saturday, September 25th, 2004 at 4:30 a.m., my water broke. I freaked out! For months, I had tried to mentally prepare myself for this moment, but when it actually arrived, I was terrified. I woke up my brother and told him to tell my dad while I phoned the hospital. I was told to come in immediately. I called my boyfriend, who drove me and my dad to the University of Washington Medical Center. At 8:08 p.m., after nearly sixteen hours of labor, Brianna was born.

Often teen mothers do not return to school. That wasn't the case for me. Instead, I returned to school after Brianna was born, and found myself locked in a battle for my education. The teen parent program had a different teacher that year, one who neglected her duty to teach and was absent 108 of the 180 days of school.

We had twenty-four different substitutes, and many times we were left with no teacher at all. We were given assignments we had already done, or we would watch the same movies over and over. On many occasions students were left to create their own assignments and projects. We were asked to work on projects that were inappropriate for the ages of our children, such as me reading books on toddlers when my daughter was still a newborn.

Most high school students might welcome a chance to not have homework or class work, but not me. The teen parenting class was supposed to help us locate resources and give us information pertaining to being a young parent. Not receiving any education at all was unacceptable to me. So I wrote letters. I started out by writing simple but formal complaints to the principal of the school. I thought the principal would do something about this problem. I was wrong.

After writing many letters to the principal, and fed up with the lack of results, I located the mailing address for his boss and began writing letters to him. Once more, nothing happened. I wondered who could I write to that cared about the students and would be outraged that something like this was going on. Then it hit me. I wrote to the superintendent of the Seattle School District. Surely he would care. But no, he didn't. In fact nothing would come of those letters until later in my junior year.

My sophomore year ended and my junior year was fast to come. The summer flew by and before I knew it, I was sitting in class again. The previous teacher of the teen parent program no longer taught at the school. Instead, Audra was back. Audra is not only a great teacher who cares about her students, but she is a wonderful person. Having her there was not only a relief, but a godsend.

Brianna was getting so big! She had just turned one and was walking everywhere. She had been rather bald as an infant so I was stoked that she was finally starting to get some hair. She was growing so fast, I couldn't believe it. Time really does fly, as did my junior year. That year I participated in the 826 Seattle book project, *It's Not Always Happily Ever After*, and even got a picture in the paper because of it. In fact it was when I was being interviewed by Cara Solomon of *The Seattle Times* for the 826 project that she mentioned she had heard of me and wanted to interview me about my issues with Marshall.

We met for coffee at Starbucks up on Capitol Hill a few weeks later. She told me she was interested in writing a story about Marshall and was wondering what my feelings were about the school. I told her everything, truthfully. I told her that I went an entire school year without learning anything of substance in my parenting class. I told her about the effort I put into trying to change that. I told her about all the letters I wrote and that I never received any responses. I told her how it saddened me to see such a fine program go to waste for so long and no one doing anything about it. She listened intently, took her notes, and occasionally asked a question. When the meeting ended she told me she would be getting in touch with me soon. It was months before I heard back from her.

Before long, it was summer again. And what an eventful summer it was! I went back to Selah to visit friends, and my daughter went with my father to Quincy to see my grandmother. I was away from Brianna for a week, the longest I ever have been. When I saw her again, I swore she grew a foot. While most of my friends were out partying, or doing what teenagers do that summer, I was at home or at the park playing with my little girl. It never bothered me that I could no longer do the things my friends did. Brianna is my world; seeing her smile or hearing her laugh is way better then anything else.

At the beginning of my senior year Brianna had her second birthday. Now let me tell you, what they say about terrible two's is all true. Brianna went from a handful to two handfuls; I guess one for each year of her life. But along with all the hassles of raising a toddler, there are also the perks. Brianna began talking more and her knowledge and curiosity far surpasses her little body.

Another milestone that year was my participation in the Running Start program. Instead of taking classes at Marshall, I went to a nearby community college where my credits doubled as both high school and college credits. I love it. I am more challenged in college then I could ever be at Marshall.

Of all the things of my senior year, said to be the most memorable year of high school, what I will remember most is when I finally received the call from Cara Solomon of *The Seattle Times*. The story about Marshall was going to be published and she wanted to know a good time for a photographer to come and take pictures of my daughter and me. A week later on December 11, 2006, "One school's legacy: 'There's no learning'" made the front page of *The Seattle Times*.

I couldn't believe it! I read the story and looked at the picture of me and Brianna on the front page, and it was a gratifying moment. All the frustration I went through, all the effort, all of the hours wasted in parenting class during my sophomore year, was now available for the world to read. I had worked so hard in my struggle for an education and now the world knew. I am proud of that article.

Even though I have received criticism from some of the teachers at Marshall, I stood up for what I believed in. It took two years for someone to notice but it was well worth it. I am a role model for my daughter and I want her growing up knowing that she should stand up for what's right. Even to the discontent of many at Marshall, I still walk the halls with my head held high.

So behind all the data and all the numbers and all the statistics, there is me. Teen mothers, like everything and everyone, are stereotyped and forced to live with stigmas. I chose to break away from that mold, a step which is hard, but not as difficult as it's made out to be. If it wasn't for my daughter, who knows where I would be. I am no longer on drugs or ditching school. Because of her, my focus is on bettering myself and making sure she has a great life.

I have worked extremely hard and I have unleashed strengths inside myself that I didn't know I had. And while I have struggled, I believe that anyone can do anything they set their minds to do. Being a teen mom isn't a burden I am forced to live with, it is a blessing that I cherish. No matter what life throws at you, you are only a failure if you choose to be.

I chose my life. I chose to be a mother. It is the best decision I have ever made.

Author's Note

There are many people who were there for me and continue to be. I am not able to mention everyone because that would turn my short story into a long book.

I would like to say thank you to my boyfriend, Mike, who never complained about late night feedings or dirty diapers. He has stood by my side through everything and continues to play a loving role in my life, as well as the life of our daughter. (See Dad, I told you so.)

To Ms. Audra, who is always there to offer her support and make sure that I am all right.

To the staff at the Marshall daycare, who have watched Brianna grow with me, offered great advice, and given me invaluable resources.

To my father, who through all of his hardships is still a loving grandparent with a golden heart, no matter what anyone says.

Thanks to my brother, Jon, who has been to hell and back with me and continues to be my rock.

And lastly, to my mother. Even though we've had our tough times and haven't seen each other in years, she raised me right. She has given me the foundation I have to be a great mother and I will always love her for that.

Eighteen-year-old **Kathy Graves** finds inspiration in her two-and-a-half-year-old daughter, Brianna. When she and Brianna aren't playing together, Kathy enjoys writing and hanging out with friends. Her goals include graduating from high school in June and continuing her education. She considers herself determined, dedicated, and empathetic.

THE WAY I SEE THINGS
IS THAT WHATEVER
HAPPENS, GOOD OR BAD,
HAPPENS FOR A REASON.

Are We There Yet?
Collin Richter

Of all the places I've lived, Renton is my favorite because I lived there with my dad. I liked the area, I was in a school I enjoyed, and I was with people like me. One time a couple of my friends came over and we blasted Slipknot out of my dad's stereo and started a five-person mosh pit, including my dad. When I had to move, I was upset, because I wanted to live with my dad, not my mom.

Renton wasn't the first place I lived. My life has been full of changes. I have lived in seventeen different homes and attended ten different schools. I've lived with my dad separately, with my mom separately, and with them both together. Although I have been through all of these moves, I'm glad it all happened because otherwise I wouldn't be who I am today and I wouldn't know the people I know.

For four years I lived in Wellpinit, Washington, with my mom, dad, and brother. My dad got in big trouble with the law. All I remember is waking up to my mom and grandma dragging my older brother and me out of the house, saying we had to move to Grandma's for a little while. I didn't realize why they were in such a hurry, but later my dad told me a story of FBI vehicles surrounding the house.

While living for two months with my grandma, I visited all of my mom's side of the family. It was nice to see them but I was wondering why I wasn't with my dad and what was going on. I visited my dad every other week, which was cool, but I wanted to live with him.

After living with my grandma, my mom, brother, and I moved into an apartment building in Colville when I was five. I made a couple of new friends but it didn't last long because my mom and dad got back together again and we rented a small house in Spokane. The area wasn't the best, but it was a nice house. My dad bought a gray/silver 1985 Mercedes Benz. The car was nice, but somebody blew it up with some kind of explosive. It was about a dispute my dad was in. My whole family woke up to a loud noise and when we went to see what it was my dad opened the front door to the sight of our car in flames. After this incident we had to move, because my mom feared there might be drive-by shootings.

We moved to another place in Spokane where the area was a little bit better and our house was a lot bigger. I enjoyed living there, and made some friends, and got involved in going to church on Sundays. One bad thing about the house was that it was infested with spiders and, as a six-year-old, they scared me because if you got bit by one, you could get a bad infection.

Later on, my mom and dad split up again, so we had to move, but this time I lived with my dad. My brother and I moved with my dad to Carnation to live with my aunt and uncle. Living with other family members was a good experience.

I was always with my cousins, but we didn't go to school together. They went to a Jewish private school and my brother and I went to a Carnation public school. It was fun celebrating Hanukkah with them, although I'm not Jewish. After a while my mom and dad got back together again so we moved to an apartment building in Issaquah.

Issaquah was a nice place to live. There were no worries and life was carefree. My mom and dad both worked at the same job at CD Express. Sometimes I would help build CD cases for a nickel each. A nickel might not have been much money, but at seven I didn't really care. It was money. The apartment building was nice, the area was peaceful and it was a short distance from shopping centers. Later on my mom and dad wanted to move again, so we moved into a house deep in the forest north of North Bend.

Living there was my favorite so far. I made a lot of good friends and liked the school I was going to. I made a tree fort in my backyard with our neighbor who went to the same school I did. The fort had three stories and a little shed with a blue tarp covering it where we kept our tools and equipment and sometimes hid. We would always wander in the forest and see what we could find, and one time we found this big area clear of trees, except for the one that had fallen and provided a bench. The house was a rental until the owners moved back into Washington from Arizona, so we had to move again.

That move wasn't a big change because we were still in the same area, so my brother and I kept our friends this time. We still attended North Bend Elementary but I was nine, so I went up a grade. Also living here we made more friends who lived in the same apartment complex and went to the same school, so the move was a good one this time. Every day we would come home from school and ride bikes and play cops and robbers or other active games. But a problem about living in North Bend was that I never saw my dad because he got too involved in work.

The next move was to Fall City. I didn't like the house in Fall City. It was nice and big, which was cool, but it was really old. The place was infested with rats and the plumbing needed a lot of work. Another reason why I hated this place is that it was around this time my mom and dad got divorced. I consider myself lucky, though, because some parents get divorced when their kids are a lot younger than ten. While my dad went to a rehab institution, my brother and I moved in with my grandma back in Spokane.

Moving back to Spokane was cool, and so was living with my

dad's side of the family. Occasionally my mom and dad would come, separately, to visit. At the end of the school year my dad came over to Spokane and picked up my brother and me to go and live with him in Renton. Life was best while living in Renton with my dad. I met a lot of cool people and good friends who lived close by and went to school with me. I made a really good friend living in this area who is still my friend today, which is rare because of all the moves I went through. Almost every day my dad, brother, and I went swimming and rafting in a lake near our house. It was the first time in my eleven years of life that we had a weekly activity as a family.

My mom and dad went to custody court and my mom won, so my brother and I had to move with her to Kenmore. This was a huge move for me because I didn't want to live with my mom instead of my dad, but I adapted to the area really well. Also, for the first time in my life, I loved the school I was going to. But I hated the fact that we had to move from our school and friends, and mostly I hated that I wasn't living with my dad anymore.

At first the Kenmore apartment was a dream come true. The area was really scenic, there were weightlifting machines, a pool and hot tub in the complex, and the buildings were new, but later on we found out that most of the neighbors were drug addicts. My brother and I still attended Kenmore Junior High, where we met more people. While living here, my mom had to be sent to Alcoholics Anonymous because of her three DUIs, so she completely quit drugs and alcohol and life became a lot easier. My mom thought this area was a bad environment for her sobriety, so we had to move again, to another place in Kenmore.

This new place was a condo. We hadn't lived in one so far, so it was a different experience. The condo slowly fell apart while we lived there, and my family was losing respect for the place the longer we stayed. Our nice new home turned into a disaster, so we moved again, this time to our current location in downtown Seattle.

The apartment in Seattle is really old and I didn't want to move in, but it was the only place we could afford in the area where my mom wanted to live. She wanted a whole new change, so we started out fresh with everything new. The apartment looked really nice when we moved in and got all of our new furnishings in place, but just like all the other homes this place is slowly falling apart.

In the future we are moving to Texas.

What I have learned from all these moves is that life is full of changes and there's nothing I can really do about it, so I have to deal with it. I don't really know how I feel about the whole thing but I can imagine it has benefited me more than harmed me because without all the moves I wouldn't be as easily adaptable to changes. I have learned to socialize and make new friends. The way I see things is that whatever happens, good or bad, happens for a reason. I have learned from my experiences and I've been to hell and back, so I always tell myself, "People in hell need their ice water and I'm the one to bring it to them."

Fourteen-year-old **Collin Richter** describes himself as "active." He enjoys hanging out with people, eating chips and drinking Coke, and listening to music by the band Slipknot, which he considers an inspiration. Collin's goal is to become employed and earn at least $50,000 a year. About this book project, he says, "I didn't know if I wanted to do it at first, but I was glad I was doing it while writing."

I WAS ABOUT TO START
ALL OVER WITH MY MAMA
AND THAT'S ALL I NEEDED
RIGHT ABOUT THEN: LOVE
FROM MY MAMA.

Get Away
Akeisha Deloach

Has there ever been a day when you wished you were someone else and had their life? I remember when that day was for me.

I was on my way home from school in the C.D. (Central District) and had to go all the way to Renton. I had already missed my first bus and I knew my dad was going to trip, but not the way he did. I was sitting with my home girl Miranda at the bus stop gossiping about anyone we knew. When my bus finally came I told her I would see her after school the next day. When I finally made it home I had to knock on the door because I left my key in my room.

Knock, knock...ring, ring...knock, knock. When I saw my dad come down the stairs I was glad someone was there because all I wanted to do was go in my room and relax because I didn't have any homework. My dad opened the door.

"What are you doing here?" he asked me

Thinking he was playing, I said, "I live here."

"No you don't," he tells me. "Get off my property or I will call the police." There was rage in his voice. "Go back where you was at with whoever you were with, because you're not staying here anymore. Bye."

All because I was forty-five minutes late. So I was like, forget it, and started back to the bus stop. As I was walking, all kinds of things were running through my head, like, where am I gonna stay? How was I gonna eat? I was thinking, I'm all by myself now.

So I thought for a real long time as to where I was going to stay, and before the bus came I decided to go over to Miranda's house in the South End until I could find someone close to stay with. So I caught the bus back to the C.D., and from the C.D. to Rainier Beach. When I got to Miranda's house I told her and her mom what happened, and she said I could stay as long as I wanted to. After Miranda showed me where to put my things she asked if I was hungry. "Hecky yeah, I'm hungry." She laughed at me and said, "Come on." We left her house, got on the bus to Rainier Beach and got some burgers. On our way back to Miranda's house she asked me if I had a boyfriend.

"No," I said, "do you?"

"Yes," she told me. "His name is Cris and he's tall, about five-foot-eleven, has brown skin with really good hair and a body like Omarion," she said, real geek.

"How old is he?" I asked.

"He's seventeen."

"Does he know how old you are?"

"Yes," she said, and told me that I would meet him soon.

It had been about four days since I got put out, and Miranda and I were real close. Her mama liked having me around, so Miranda was like, "Why don't you ask your dad, can we adopt you?" I thought about it and it sounded good to me because I was used to doing me when I wanted to. Later on that day I called my dad and asked him, and he told me yeah, but if you know my dad, you know he wouldn't just let some stranger take his kids. I told him all right, then hung up the phone and told Miranda and her mama what he said. Miranda was so happy, and we started calling each other sisters.

We stopped going to school because Miranda was suspended and the police were looking for me, because my dad called the police after I left and told them that I ran away, and that he didn't know why. But spring break was starting anyway. Later on, Miranda and I went to my aunt's house. When we got there she asked me why I wasn't at home. I told her everything, even about the adoption.

"Why don't he let family adopt you?" she asked.

"I don't know," I told her. After she lectured me on being out in the streets, she hugged me and kissed me good-bye and told me to be safe, and Miranda and I left.

By the time we made it to Miranda's house we were hella tired, so we fell out once again, and when I woke up, there was this sexy black god who I thought came to save me from this thing I was living called life. When Miranda introduced him as Cris, all that stopped, and I was sick about it.

"Hey, how you doin?" I asked him, trying to be happy.

"Aight," he said. Then he and Miranda went out the door and left me there by myself. Not too long after they left I was asleep again, having dreams about the sexy god that I knew now I would never have, then BOOM! the front door shut and Miranda and Cris walked back in.

"Girl you been asleep this whole time since we left?" she asked me.

"Um, let me think. Uh, yeah. You two left with out saying bye or nothing."

"My bad," she said, laughing. The stuff wasn't funny at all to me, but I let it go.

Miranda had plans to go over to her dad's house for the weekend, and I wasn't up to it, but she insisted that I go with her because I would be doing nothing, so I went.

You know how they say you should follow your first mind? Whoever made that saying was right, because I should have. When Miranda's dad came to get us, he asked a lot of questions about who I was, and Miranda told him everything that happened those last couple of weeks. He told me that it was not good for me to be there with them because her mom was never there, and that I needed to go home. He said he would take me after the weekend was over. When we were on our way, I was so mad at the thought of going back to that place it made my stomach hurt. When we made it to the house, I was mad to be there too, knowing that when I left that I would be going back home—some place I didn't want to go. The time I spent at Miranda's dad's house was fun, and sometimes I would forget that I was going home after the weekend, but every time I looked at the clock it would remind me how much time I had left.

Sunday finally came, and I had a lump in my throat so big I thought that I wouldn't be able to swallow. Too bad that lump wasn't big enough to kill me. When we pulled up to my house, I felt the pain in my stomach and I had a bad feeling about being there again. As I walked up to the door, my dad's wife Tracy was already opening it. She thanked Miranda's dad for bringing me home, then she shut the door.

SMACK! I fell to the floor and felt a hard kick in my ribs. I tried to get up the stairs as fast as I could to get away from her but she was right on me, kicking and punching anywhere she felt could hurt me. When I made it to my room I was so mad that I was so ready to go toe-to-toe with her the next blow she took. I would have to retaliate fast and hard. Just as I thought she would, she came into my room as I was putting things away. She started to cuss me out and called me a type of name and that just added fuel to the fire. After what seemed like an hour of her ranting and raving, she tried to strike me once more, but I was ready this time and I let her have it. POW! Right in the gut. She curled over, and she really started cussing me out. Then, when she gained her composure she told me to take off my belt. I told her no, because she did not buy it for me, and that's when she slapped me right smack dab in the face. Holding my face, I began to take off my belt and give it to her. Just as I was about to hand it to her I tried to whack her one real good with it so she would leave me alone, but to my surprise she caught it and snatched it from me, and I knew that it was a wrap. She beat me until I cried out to my mama to come and rescue me from this evil lady who my dad called his wife. When she left my room to let me cry by myself she told me that she didn't want anything to do with me, and that she would tell my dad what happened and hope that he put me out again. She said that if I wanted to leave I could go right now without anything but the clothes on my back.

That night when my dad came home from work he was so angry at me that he couldn't even find the words to tell me how he felt about the whole situation, but I knew, and that's what made me want to leave again the next day. As planned, I left that morning when everyone had gone to work and school. As I walked out, I turned to look at the house that once was filled with love and so many emotions, knowing this would be the last time I would see it. I ended up going back to Miranda's house for a few more days, and that's when it hit me. I needed more than just a home, I needed love. Love from a family of my own, and not one that I shared.

Three days after staying at Miranda's house I split to go back home. On my way back there were no buses running my way, so I went downtown to chill and see if I could find anyone I knew. Sure enough, I saw this girl I went to school with named Brook, and her mama had put her out too. We were on our way to find out how we were going to survive in the streets. Lucky for us we ran into her cousin who told us that we could stay with him for a while, so that's where we went. The next day we went downtown to go shopping, because Brook's cousin gave us some money to spend, and I was not about to turn down money, with the predicament I was in.

Downtown, Brook and I shopped a little here and there and everywhere, but we went to a store that was way too rich for our blood. Brook decides to go take a look and see could she afford anything. She knew she couldn't, but she went in anyway. When she found that she didn't have enough money to buy anything, she went to the dressing room to try on the jogging suit she wanted so badly. When she came out she didn't have it anymore and I thought she probably had left it in the dressing room. On our way out the door I felt a strong hand grab my arm and a voice say not to panic, and to follow him to the back. I did as I was told, not knowing what was going on. Then I remembered Brook's jogging suit.

They led Brook and me to a really small, dimly lit room in the back of the store and told us to tell them where the jogging suit was, and not to lie because they had us on video. They said they knew that we stole various items, and that they needed to check our bags. I let them check my bags without hesitation, but some of the stuff they pulled out I didn't remember picking up. My mind went blank, and all I could think was, I'm going to jail because of Brook. After they searched us and removed the items that weren't paid for, they asked us our names and everything, and they asked who could we call to come and get us. Her cousin who had given us the money couldn't come to get us, because he had warrants and would have gone straight to jail. So we had no choice but to tell them the truth, that we were living on the streets.

We ended up going to the Spruce Street Crisis Residential Center and they were cool there, but it was still like jail. We had to clean, eat, and sleep when they said so, but when we did have our free time it was fun. After three days there I was transferred to a group home, because they said that's what had to happen if someone didn't come to get you. When I first saw the home it was like a mini mansion, with four floors. It didn't look as bad as I expected. I was kind of happy to be there, because they had lots to do, I had my own room, and the other kids there were real cool.

I was getting used to living there, but then they called me to the office and told me that my case manager had tracked down my mother, who was living in Detroit. They gave me a ticket to Detroit, and I was so ecstatic that I started to cry a little. I was finally going to see my mama, after all that I had been through. I was going to make sure that I told her everything about me and what happened to me, and find out why she left me and let all that horrible stuff happen to me.

After they told me I would be leaving the next day, I ran to my room to pack all my things and waited. As soon as I went to sleep was as soon as the morning came. I was up and ready to go with no regret about any of the decisions that I made those past couple of weeks that I'd been on my own. I was about to start all over with my mama and that's all I needed right about then: love from my mama. On my way to the airport I was thinking about all that I've been through and it was well worth it to me, and how I was ready for what was to come next in my life.

When my plane touched down in Detroit, I was taken back to a place that I forgot had existed. I felt like everything that I wanted and more was right there in Detroit. I had stayed with Mama many times before over the years, so it felt like coming home to me. When I got to my mama, I cried for a long time in her arms as she held me and told me it was going to be all right. When we got to the house, I was in awe at how hood it was. I always liked stuff that was hood, hood boys, home, school, and just the hood itself. It made me feel welcomed to a part of me that had been missing all fourteen years of my life. When we got in the house, I hugged my sisters and little brothers and my auntie, and my mama introduced me to my brother's daddy and left that at that. I was real tired, but my sister asked me to go outside with her on the porch, even though it was 11:00 p.m. I was up to it, to see who I could see.

After about a month there I was really used to the way I was living. The whole atmosphere had my adrenalin rushing and had me geeked all the time, and as days passed I got closer and closer to my mama, and that's exactly where I wanted to be. I spent four great years in Detroit with my mama, and we got as close as close can get. She made me remember what love is and how to give it back to someone who wants it and needs it. And it was nice to be with family that acted just like me, liked some of the same things I like, and was just there for me. I loved being with my mama. She was the only person I knew who was just like me, and I feel like I am a lot like her. It just goes to show you that there's nothing like motherly love, right?

Now I'm back in Seattle. After all the years I've been away, now here I am back to square one, but this time I'm with someone who wants to be with me: my mama and my brothers and sisters—the family I love.

"If I weren't me, but someone else who met me, I would love me," says seventeen-year-old **Akeisha Deloach**, who hopes you'll love her story. She thinks this book project could be the big break she needs to get her stories out. In addition to writing, Akeisha loves reading and listening to music. And, if she could sing, she says would do that, too.

DON'T FIGHT HIM, BE
ACCEPTING.
NOTHING'S HAPPENING
THAT YOU'RE NOT
LETTING.

Why Does He Stalk Me So?
Asuzena Rodriguez

Life and change, change and life. Two peas in a pod, inseparable. These two things are always together and will always be together. Everyone lives a life and everyone goes through adjustments. Maybe not dramatic ones, but everyone has gone through some kind of modification that has altered life in some way. Permanently, possibly not, but change in life is almost inevitable.

Change, never a friend of mine
But I'm stuck with him till the end of time.

He never leaves, never lets me be.
I want things to stay the same

BURNING THE PAST

I want my life forever tame.

Not wild, unpredictable, and fickle
But life unchanged is unreal.
He remains inside me, sealed.

He's always there, in the back of my mind

As you might know, possibly foresee
Tickling me from the inside.

He isn't only with me

He's with you, too.
You can feel him now, can't you?

Don't fret; he's been there all along

Not always heard, like a far off song.
Don't fight him, be accepting.

Nothing's happening that you're not letting.

You can't trick him, beat him, or win against him.
He's been there for a while;

You're nothing he can't handle,

So lick him, stick him, tape him to your backpack
'Cause when he comes around, everything you know

is *never* coming back.

"Come on, what kind of question is this?" sixteen-year-old **Asuzena Rodriguez** says, when asked about this book project. "Of course everyone thinks it's awesome or they wouldn't be doing it! I mean how many high school students can say they wrote something in a published book?" Asuzena likes to draw, write short stories, and make the people around her happy. She loves her own weirdness, and she is inspired by her best friend Christine, whom she calls "my backbone to life."

I DIDN'T WANT THE
MAINSTREAM LIFE, THE
NICE CARS, THE BIG
HOUSES, LIKE AN OLD
TV SHOW.

Meeting on a Heavy Branch
Trevor Jones

Out of the house, out of school—the world isn't the same place it used to be. Three years ago it wasn't like this at all. I used to be the preppy kid at the rich school, with the good friends and the semi-mild parents, the good life of the normal kid.

Then I started hanging out with some of the punk rocker kids so I could see how it was being in a different group; I was looking for a change. I didn't want to be the preppy kid with no cool friends. The new group I started to hang with was a particularly nasty group, doing drugs and bullying other kids. They wore a violently dark shade of grey, long greasy hair, and tight pants. I felt more powerful with them, and I felt in control. That's when my life started to change.

Instead of having a good reputation, I started to act like a dropout (skipping school and doing what drugs I could find), and hanging with the dropouts. I started to party with my friends. I was lacking the required grades needed to pass, and I couldn't get a grip on my actions, even though I could control others' actions in school.

My parents got divorced around the same time I started to hang with the new crowd, and my dad became a less important factor in my life for a while, because I just saw him on the weekends. I started living with my mom, but I couldn't get into the loving mother I once had. For some reason, she was now acting like the Wicked Witch of the West from the Wonderful Wizard of Oz, and she would yell at me for countless things. Some of those things would include whether I had more homework to do, or whether I ate enough food, believe it or not. Did I mention that I was fat?

My dad re-entered my immediate life by taking a more active role (he wanted me to live with him, but I didn't), and he had a whole other way of dealing with the breakup than my mom did. Instead of yelling at me, he would teach me to do things, and take me places I would have never gone to alone. He took me to rock concerts, like the Mars Volta, and underground artists that have since broken up. He taught me how to ride a scooter, and he also taught me to skateboard, which kept me out of the house and helped me to lose weight. He saw how unhappy I was with my life, having no friends because my mom wouldn't let me do things with other kids in fear that she might "lose me" to the other children's parents. With his permission, I'd go to their houses more often. He let me have friends over, and he would let me go over to their houses on a daily basis. These actions that he got me into doing made me feel great, and I could finally enjoy the outdoors like I could never before.

But things started to get crazy out-of-control with my mom (she was starting to try to control me), and my grades started dropping even more. I became clinically depressed. I knew I was depressed, because I started to eat more than I used to, and I wasn't as social with other people. I couldn't find the will to be around other people because of my home life. Depression felt like I was in a dark room, with nothing in it except the smell of rotting flesh and beached fish.

Finally, things got better when she started seeing this guy named

Tim. Tim changed me in a way I liked, and got me out of depression. He would take me to the airfield, and he taught me how to do the things I enjoyed watching on TV, like flying remote controlled airplanes, and racing remote controlled cars. He helped me get into the electronics field of interest, and actually inspired me to do what I want to do for a living. He inspired me to be a musician, and work in a studio recording records for other artists. He got me interested in this by taking me to the actual studios, and having me watch recording being done. It was cool, with all the machines and instruments.

However, things didn't stay smooth. Tim had to move to Kentucky for his work (he got a raise and took it), so my mom wasn't able to remain happy. She started to cry a lot again, which again impacted my school life, and I was being yelled at more. I still talk to him (don't let my mom know, she will flip), and he hooks me up with DJs at raves.

When I got to middle school the next year at Alderwood Middle School, my life changed even more radically. I had more reason to be free, since I was growing up finally, so my mom couldn't keep her iron grip on me, and my dad asked if I wanted to do things with my old friends instead of just sitting around and playing video games. I made more friends, and unfortunately, some of them were bad influences. They got me into trying out some bad things, like even harder drugs and alcohol. My grades started to drop once again, and I was in lots of trouble with the law. My parents didn't like my friends even though they were a little milder than my previous friends.

I wasn't really wanted in my mom's house (she'd gotten remarried), because I now had a stepdad and a new stepbrother. My mom didn't want me to put a negative influence on my older stepbrother, because he was her ideal form of the child she wanted so badly for her own. I was an outcast from the family, and cursed by everyone because I was a punk skater, and my mom's family was full of beauty contestant material. I wasn't a straight-A student, and I didn't fit in.

My life seemed like it was getting me nowhere, because I was still partying more than doing schoolwork. Even with my new friends, I still had control over people, but even less over myself. I still went on partying with my less known friends in school (the punks), and also the posse I was generally seen with (the ravers). I moved in with my stepdad and mom during the summer of this year because my mom had married him, and went to a school known as Edmonds Woodway. Edmonds was supposed to be a new start for me, according to my mom, who was still trying to transform me into a snob.

I didn't want the mainstream life, the nice cars, the big houses, like an old TV show ("Everybody Loves Raymond" and "The Brady Bunch"). I had seen what those people are like, with their noses in the air to the poorer crowds. I just kept doing my thing by going to raves and smoking, and eventually got into more trouble and illegal things, and started getting suspended.

I got kicked out of my mom's house and moved in with my dad, and now I go to John Marshall Alternative School. So far things are going better for me. I'm getting a new start at life like I needed. I went from a rich neighborhood with fancy BMWs and lots of snobby kids to a run-down brick apartment with lots of friendly middle-class neighbors, and I think it's going to be a better experience for me. I learned that even though people are always aiming for the high life, I didn't do too well up there, and some personalities aren't made for that kind of life. This is my story.

"Gotta get a running start somewhere," says fifteen-year-old **Trevor Jones**, when asked how he feels about this book project. "Why not here?" You can find Trevor skating, raving, and hanging out with his friends Tom and PJ, who are his inspirations. His goals include becoming a DJ and landing a fun job.

IT WAS THE FIRST TIME
I HAD ACTUALLY STOOD
UP FOR MYSELF.

There's One Way to Handle Things
Steven McAlpin

People always say, "If you don't pay attention to bullies, they will leave you alone." But, in my experience, they still don't.

In the third grade I lived in Reno, Nevada, and I was getting picked on. I ignored the bully, which is what my teachers said to do, but I still complained left and right. My mom talked to the school, but with no results. I was happy that this bully was in sixth grade and left at the end of the year.

The next year another bully came and pushed me in the halls, hit me, and took my lunch money. His name was Alberto. It felt like it would always be the same thing all over again. I was in fourth grade, Alberto was in the fifth, and I had two years of this before he left.

One day Alberto started pushing me up against the locker, and for the first time I had enough courage to push him back. He punched me in the face and then I pretty much went crazy. I started beating him uncontrollably. I couldn't stop; nothing was holding me back now. The teachers had to break up the fight by pulling us apart. It was the first time I had actually stood up for myself.

In the seventh grade I moved to Las Vegas and it started again. I got bullied a lot, so I complained and put notes in the bully box (a place where you could write notes to alert the teachers about bullying), but nothing happened. One day, six boys jumped me. I still have a scar on my arm where one of the kid's ring cut my skin. The next week, I showed up to school and people were staring at me. About two hours later, I was told that one of the kids that jumped me had brought a gun and a knife to shoot or stab me. He was arrested for reckless endangerment and carrying a gun without a license.

The next week, his friends came to jump me. They surrounded me, but this time I was prepared. I took out the smallest guy first and worked my way up. They didn't mess with me again.

My mom decided that we would move north. We moved to Kirkland, then Seattle, and here I am at John Marshall Alternative School.

People always say, "If you don't pay attention to bullies they will leave you alone." You make your own decision, but it didn't work that way for me. What are we going to do?

If you need a good excuse, look to thirteen-year-old **Steven McAlpin**. He describes himself as cool, smart, and a good excuse-maker. He loves to play video games and various sports, and hopes to play in the NFL some day (or become a rapper). What inspires Steven most? His family, he says.

I KNOW THERE ARE
GOING TO BE A LOT OF
CHALLENGES FOR ME
IN A REGULAR SCHOOL,
BUT I CAN'T JUST AVOID
IT BY STAYING HERE.

Reality Check
Devonte Parson

Changing from Washington Middle School to John Marshall Alternative School impacted my life. Not only in where I went to school but also in my personality and my ways.

In the sixth grade I started at Washington Middle School hearing about the big bad teachers working there. It never scared me, though. I'm the type of kid who likes to go against all authorities who think they can tell the kids what to do all the time. I looked at it this way: if you were going to be the big bad teacher, I was going to be the big bad kid. I always thought if you're telling me what to do—even though it's for my own good—you were trying to be in control of me. I don't like to feel like anyone else is in control of me.

Well, being at Washington Middle School started just how I

planned it to. The teachers were trying to scare the little kids in sixth grade early, but I wasn't going for it. I tried to scare the teachers right back with my anger. So whenever I sensed the teacher was telling me to do something in a mean way, I would flip out. I'd shove desks, throw chairs, curse, yell, and even advance menacingly toward the teachers. I would get suspended, but for some reason it felt good to me to get angry and scare the teachers. It was like the feeling you get when you achieve a goal you have been working on for years.

So after gaining what I thought was fear from the teachers, I wanted to gain popularity from the kids. I got a bunch of friends by just chilling with other kids and doing dumb stuff with them. I then began to get suspended on a daily basis. I was only attending school about two weeks out of each month. I always showed up and did all of my work well, but I got done with it too fast. I would be so bored when I didn't have anything else to do, I'd get on the teacher's nerves for passing time.

One day the vice principal took me into his office because I missed one week of a three-week lunchtime detention. He wanted to call my grandma, but I didn't want him to. He called anyway. Anger rushed to my head and I flashed and started cursing at him and knocking stuff onto the floor. He told me to stop before things escalated.

I shouted, "No!" and then I said I wished the school would just burn down. He took it as a threat. I was emergency expelled, immediately.

After my month of emergency expulsion I came back to school to bask in my fame. Everyone was coming up to me and asking why I did it, even the people that weren't at school on that day. It made me feel like a star in a weird way.

I didn't notice how dumb my decisions were until I was placed in an anger management class inside the school. That is when things first started to change.

After my first month in that class, I learned that you could never be the worst kid around. There were kids in that class who were angrier than me, and for smaller things. My teacher was a heavyset man who'd worked on death row for some years. I could not punk the teacher like I thought I would be able to. If you were angry and advanced toward him in a violent way, well I'd wish you the best of luck. I kept trying and trying to scare him, but it just wouldn't work.

There were things that I liked about that class, too. If you did your work and were good, you were able to earn progress points. With the progress points you were able to buy snacks from the cupboard in our room that we called "the store." Another thing about being in that class is you were respected. Whenever you walked down the hall you would get handshakes and people saying, "What's up," people you never even thought about talking to before. You would still get into fights but it wasn't as likely to happen as opposed to being a regular student. I guess when you have anger problems not many people want to make you angry.

One day a teacher asked me where my hall pass was. I told the teacher I didn't have one. The teacher then told me to go to in-school suspension. I blew up fast and grabbed the nearest object, a chair. I launched the chair at the teacher. They called the police and I was handcuffed in front of all of the kids in the school. Then I was escorted five blocks away and told to walk home.

I was emergency expelled again. This time when I came back it was to have a meeting to determine my placement. They had a meeting with my grandma and all of the teachers there. They decided that I would be expelled and put into John Marshall Alternative School. I had heard things about Marshall so I prepared myself to punk the teachers there, too.

My first week at Marshall was crazy for me. I saw kids get angry and launch at teachers. Going from a school with teachers that talked gentle to you when you got angry and got scared when you knocked things down, to another school where they didn't, and where kids were ten times worse than you, was one of the biggest changes in my life. I had never been to a school where I was aware of kids who were worse than me.

At Marshall, the third floor is the behavioral problem floor. There's the first floor re-entry and the second floor re-entry. Those programs are just like a regular high school and middle school; it's just that you're in an alternative school. The third floor is where you stay in one class all day. You can't transition from one room to another without a staff person having to follow you. People often mistake the third floor as a place for retarded kids, but it's not. Most kids on the third floor only have anger problems and fight a lot. One thing about Marshall, when you are the new kid on the third floor you get messed with if nobody knows you. I had never been in a fight inside of school in my life until I got to Marshall. In my first five months there I got into three fights.

I didn't start getting the hang of being a third floor student at Marshall until my eighth grade year. I started making friends and it got easier. I noticed that during the time I was around the kids my attitude was changing, too. I didn't act as dumb as I did when I was going to Washington. I was still doing stupid things to annoy the teachers, but not the kids.

My goal was to get out of Marshall and go back to Washington. I set the goal for myself and had a lot of teachers helping me behind the scenes. I got to take some of my classes on the other floors. But when I was close to getting out, the old Devonte came back. I got angry with a teacher for fussing at me for tardiness. I cursed the teacher out and knocked things onto the floor. All of my classes were taken back and I was on the third floor for the full day once again.

I gave up on myself after that. I was getting restrained and put into in-school detention every day. My relationships with the teachers started turning negative because of my behavior. Every teacher on the third floor was disappointed in me. At the end of the eighth grade I looked at myself as a failure.

Then my ninth grade year came and the teachers decided to give me another chance. I was so happy but I really didn't believe in myself. I didn't understand why there were still teachers who believed in me. I came in this year with a whole different mindset though. I want out really bad. I have never been to a regular high school, and I do not want to graduate from an alternative one.

When I got my first two classes off the third floor, I was doing real good. Then I got another one and I started to fall off a little bit. Next I got the last two classes and everyone started noticing that my behavior was deteriorating. The reason was, I started to not believe it was really happening. Most of the time anything good happened to me, it usually ended up turning bad, or was in a good dream.

Every time I fall off, there is someone there to tell me I can do it. Actually, there are a few people, and they know who they are. I really want to get out of this school so I can be with all of my friends. I know there are going to be a lot of challenges for me in a regular school, but I can't just avoid it by staying here.

The people who are going to be my homies in regular school are my same homies outside of school. So I can't just duck and hide from that fact. I'm still in ninth grade at Marshall. And I now notice that all the intimidating I tried to do and all of the dumb things I did only made my situation worse. Those same teachers that I tried scaring are probably still making their money smiling. And I'm still sitting here, a student at Marshall, frowning about it all.

It's crazy because if it wasn't for writing this story, I still wouldn't understand it all, but now I do. I keep trying not to believe it, but maybe the real big change in my life was me this whole time and I just didn't want to face the facts. Well, if I expect to go anywhere, I have to go with the flow and stop running away from reality.

Fifteen-year-old **Devonte Parson** plans
to become an inspiring rapper and cites
Tupac Shakur as his own inspiration.
Devonte enjoys eating, chilling, and
making money. He considers himself
to be outgoing, funny, energetic, and
helpful, which add up to a personality
he likes a lot. He also likes this chance
to be published again (Devonte participated in last year's book project, too).

MAYBE IF SHE PUT HER
HEART INTO HER WORDS,
SHE WOULDN'T FEEL SO
ALONE LIKE SHE HAD
FOR SO LONG. MAYBE
SHE COULD GET THIS
ALL OFF HER CHEST
AND FINALLY BE HAPPY.

The Forgotten One
Carissa Muller

"I used to think of psychiatric patients as people who scream and holler, and hear voices that other people don't hear," fourteen-year-old Alice Richfield said, fumbling with a loose piece of string on her gray Old Navy sweater. "I bet you imagine that the patients have no family to visit them, that they have no pasts, no futures." She paused, wrapping the string around her fingertip. "But, that's not true. They do have pasts and futures. And they also have families that love them very much.

Alice tucked a few strands of her bottle-auburn hair behind her ear.

She had been in the school counselor's office for nearly fifteen minutes, but it seemed like forever.

"Why am I here, anyway?" she asked.

"Because, dear, I worry about you." The counselor replied, yawning quietly. "Your attendance records show you haven't been to school in three weeks, and your absences are all unexcused. Any reason why you haven't been coming?"

"Not really." Alice shrugged. "I guess I just don't like school. And I don't feel like talking about it, so don't ask."

"Anyway, have you lived with your older brother your whole life?"

Alice prepared herself. "Yeah, see, when I was about nine years old, Kurt was admitted into a psychiatric hospital. I looked up to him a lot. He influenced my outlook on life. He was, I guess you could say, my role model. I valued his opinions, and I was interested in everything he liked. We had the same tastes in music and watched the same TV shows." She paused and pulled the loose string on her sweater farther out.

"I mean, yeah, sure, we had our average brother-sister quarrels every now and then over stupid stuff, like who got to take the first shower or who got to choose which channel to watch, but I really cared about Kurt. I mean, I still do. His hospitalization really traumatized me."

Alice finally looked up from her lap. The older woman was writing on a yellow notepad. Her long gray hair was twisted up in a tight bun at the top of her head. She wore thick red glasses and a striped green and black sweater.

"Has Kurt been diagnosed with any recent mental illnesses?" she asked.

Alice nodded. "ADHD." She hesitated and said, "He's been in and out of psychiatric hospitals for the past five years. The first time was confusing. We didn't have any clue what was going on. There was even a time when I didn't get to see him for nearly a month because he wasn't mentally stable enough to be around my younger sister and me. He couldn't behave himself. He was always acting manic, and it was just too difficult for my parents to manage him."

The counselor nodded. There was a moment of awkward silence, until Alice decided to speak up again.

"They—the many psychiatrists and mental health doctors—struggled to find out what was happening to Kurt: why he was behaving so differently from all the other teenage boys his age. Eventually, the doctors settled on the idea that maybe my brother had bipolar disorder." Alice cleared her throat. "I'm sure you already know what that is, but just in case you don't, bipolar disorder is an illness where you have constant mood swings, sometimes for no reason at all. For instance, once Kurt and I were roughhousing and I accidentally hit him. He suddenly became infuriated and began yelling at me. Then, a few minutes later, he was back to normal and wanted to roughhouse again.

"Bipolar disorder isn't something that can be caught. You can't just suddenly become bipolar. You're born that way. You're always going to be bipolar, whether you're manic or depressed. That can never be changed, but with the right medication, it can be a lot easier to deal with."

"I completely understand," the counselor said.

Alice scoffed. This was the third counselor she'd been to see in the last few months, and she felt like they were all pretending to care about her. "At one point, his medications were at the right dosages, and he took them at the right times. Sure, he still had a lot of mood swings, but my family felt like it was worth it just to have him staying at home with us."

Alice thought back to the day, a couple years ago, when he was admitted to a hospital the second time. Because she had been the one to call the ambulance, she felt she had been the one who caused him to go away, that it was her fault. But she would never tell the counselor, or anyone else this because she was too ashamed of herself.

Alice's eyes began stinging with tears. She wiped her eyes and continued. "Anyway, about six months after this stable period at home, Kurt had a breakdown and attempted to... well, he tried to kill himself. Not being able to see him for a month was really hard for me, but the thought of never being able to see my brother ever again was totally devastating. My family and I were willing to give anything for him to get better. We didn't want him to lose this battle.

"So, Kurt was admitted again. This time, he stayed for eighteen long months." She frowned, and began twisting the loose piece of string around her finger again. "And this hospital was farther than the other ones. It was in Tacoma, which is about an hour's drive from

Seattle, where my family lives, so we only got to see Kurt on the weekends when he had an off-campus pass and could come home for two nights. But on Sundays he always had to go back to the hospital, and I would have to wait another five days to see him.

"Sometimes his behavior wasn't appropriate enough for him to come home without the doctor's supervision, so we had to go visit him. We would have a few short hours to eat a snack, go to the mall nearby, or take a slow walk around the hospital campus. It was upsetting when my family had to leave him there. We could tell that he desperately wanted to go home with us, and we wanted him home more than anything. It was devastating for him to live so far away.

"Even though we really wanted him to be at home for good, the doctors couldn't release him from their care if his medications weren't at the right dosage and if he couldn't handle real life situations without panicking."

Alice couldn't believe she was telling this story to a complete stranger, but she was sick and tired of bottling her feelings up. She thought that maybe if she told the counselor, she would be understood in a way she never had before. Maybe if she put her heart into her words, she wouldn't feel so alone like she had for so long. Maybe she could get this all off her chest and finally be happy.

So much attention had always been focused on Kurt that Alice practically felt as if everyone in her family had forgotten about her. Her younger sister also needed constant attention, so Alice felt her parents were so busy focusing on her siblings that they had forgotten Alice needed attention, too.

"Before Kurt was released, my family worked incredibly hard to make our household a suitable environment for Kurt. We fixed our house up, changed our schedules around so one parent would always be home to take care of him, and did everything in our power to make our house a positive environment. But according to the doctors, there was always something that needed to be corrected, such as someone's attitude or bad habit. That was upsetting. We felt like we were being told we weren't good enough.

"Finally, in July 2005, after living in different treatment facilities for so long, Kurt was released. His medications were perfect, he was stable, and we were incredibly proud of him for achieving so much. He had changed in so many ways, and we were happy that he was home."

Alice stopped talking, and there was an awkward pause for a few minutes. She pulled her feet up onto the couch she was sitting on and sat kindergarten-style, "criss-cross applesauce."

The counselor sighed. "And do you feel that you have changed as a person?"

Alice nodded. "My life has changed in so many ways. I've become a completely different person than I was when Kurt was first hospitalized. I don't see things the way that I used to. In fact, you know what? I'm not even sure if I saw things at all, because I was so used to people seeing the world for me. I feel a sense of freedom now. I can open my eyes and see the world in a brand new light: my own.

"I don't rely on Kurt or anyone else to influence me anymore. I've learned to be myself and stand up for my opinions and speak my thoughts. This whole experience has changed my personality one hundred percent." She paused for a moment, considering her words. "For example, before, when Kurt would watch a TV show, I watched it too, even though I thought it was incredibly boring. But now, I do what I want, and I'm not going to suffer to make other people happy."

The counselor smiled. "It looks like our time is up, but if you would like, you can come back for lunch tomorrow and we can talk some more."

"Sounds like a plan." Alice smiled and turned for the door.

"Alice?"

"Yeah?" she replied, turning around quickly.

"There's a group of girls who come into my office and talk about their issues. It's completely confidential, and if you would like, you could join us every Friday."

"That sounds fine, I guess," Alice said. The counselor nodded.

"Well, I better get going, I have class," Alice said quietly, reaching for the door. She stepped outside the office and silently cheered. This was the first time she had completely opened herself up to someone in years, and she was so proud of herself.

She was also proud that she no longer lived to please other people, that she was her own person. For some reason, it had just taken her a while to realize that. While she was in the counselor's office, things became much clearer. Whatever she was going to do for the rest of her life, it was up to her. She was in control, and that's the way things were going to be from now on.

What does fourteen-year-old **Carissa Muller** like most about herself? "My good taste in music." With Kurt Cobain as one of her inspirations, it's not surprising that she loves playing her guitar (along with talking on the phone, writing, and hanging out). She says that this book project "gave me a chance to do something I love." One of her goals is to write a book one day.

IF YOU PUT MY LITTLE
BROTHER AND ME IN
THE SAME ROOM YOU
WOULDN'T EVEN UN-
DERSTAND HOW WE DO
WHAT WE DO. THE WAY
WE ACT IS RIDICULOUS.

The Miracle Baby
Unique Lelonnie Que Von Rene Smith

My mother wasn't supposed to have any more kids after me. Then here he came!

Having me was a miracle for my mother being that we almost died during delivery. She was told that she wasn't going to be able to have kids, so she had me. But then the big change came eleven and a half years later.

I found out I had a little brother coming into the world in November 2000. I was ten and loving the idea of being an only child. I mean, who wouldn't want to stay spoiled? Now that's the life, don't you think? Then the day came. I can remember it as if it were yesterday. My mom had come home from her birthday trip to Las Vegas when she sprang the news on everybody that she was pregnant with twins. I was sitting down on the floor with my cousin Dellynnice playing rummy while my grandma was sitting in the chair watching us. My mom looked at me and said, "There is something I need to tell you guys."

"What?" I asked.

"I'm pregnant with twins."

You would have thought that everybody would've been overjoyed, but we were all just looking at her with stunned faces. PREGNANT! TWINS! Did you hear me? All I could do was cry. Everything was wrong; I was supposed to be an only child forever—the only one who lived with my mom. Then here she comes with this. I was shocked, just straight flabbergasted. I mean, who has another kid when their child is ten years old? I was so hurt. I really thought my mom had done something to me, when really I was just being a selfish little brat.

What followed was nine long months of an always-hungry mom. Before seeing her pregnant, I had never seen someone eat a whole watermelon by herself. Then the day finally came. It was July 16, 2001. My mom had pulled up to drop me off at my grandma's house, so I could stay there while she was in the hospital. All we saw and heard were red lights and sirens. My grandma was being taken to the hospital in the ambulance because she was having chest pains. My grandma and my mom were going to the hospital at the same time, except my mom drove herself to be admitted. You would've never thought with all the commotion made about my grandma that she would only stay in the hospital for a few hours and then be discharged. We were all just chilling at my grandma's when my mom called and said she wanted her mother up there with her when she was giving birth. So when my grandma went it seemed as if she started a stampede. And I had to stay at my grandma's house with my grandpa and my cousins.

It appeared as if everybody was up at the hospital except for me, and my feelings were hurt because I wanted to be a part of the excitement. It was like forever waiting for my mom to call or somebody to call and tell us, meaning my grandpa, Dellynnice, Randall, and me at the house, what was going on at the hospital. Then the call came. I don't remember the time exactly. I just remember it being late at night when I think my cousin Mawiyah called and told us it was a boy—seven pounds, eleven ounces. A baby brother. Wow! I was ecstatic. I kept running it through my head—a baby brother, a little bundle of joy. In the background you could hear all the commotion that everybody was making over the new baby of the family. And we were doing the same at the house.

A boy! Yup, that's what it do! I was so happy we were up all night because we were all so excited about the new baby. Did you notice that I said that it was a boy and not two beautiful, healthy boys? Well, that's because my mother lost a child during her pregnancy. I couldn't wait for my mom to come home from the hospital. I remember the day that my mom came home I had walked all the way to my grandma's house after school because she wasn't answering the door. Then I called home when I got to my grandma's house and she told me to walk all the way back so I could see the new baby. I almost ran home from my grandma's. I said almost, because my grandma lives on 23rd and East Pine and we lived on 16th and Spruce and that is so far. When I got there I couldn't wait to see him. He was so, so, so Asian-looking but cute. Don't get me wrong. He looked just like my mom in her baby pictures.

We were all happy to welcome Jay Edward into the family. But I think for my mom that was one of the hardest things in her life being that she had to deal with the fact that she lost and gained a life. To this day, I know that my mom is still dealing with the fact that she lost her baby. She told me it took forever for her to even look at twins. It was a shock to me when she lost the baby, but I really didn't understand until I had problems of my own. You might've thought I was going to be mad when he came because of the way I acted when I first found out. But I loved being an older sister. He was as cute as a button and he was mine and no one could have him, not even my mom, because I am and will always be his protector. I was going to be the one to take care of him because he is my brother and I love him.

I wouldn't let him out of my sight and he wouldn't let me out of his. When I moved, he moved, just like that. He got older and not much changed. He's like a mini me now, which isn't always good, especially when he gets mad. From diapers to boxers, he's been the apple of my eye and that'll never change. It's been about five and a half years now since he was born and although it has been hard, it has been an adventure. Just going to the park is exciting with my bobble-head bubba. To see the smile on his face warms my heart and makes my day. And he has the biggest heart; he's the sweetest kid you'll ever meet. He can see I'm crying and he'll give me a kiss on the cheek and a hug. It'll seem as if all my problems are gone for that moment.

He started kindergarten and is acting just like me, his big sister. If you put my little brother and me in the same room you wouldn't even understand how we do what we do. The way we act is ridiculous. We be having the same facial expressions, the same actions. It's almost like having a twin to me, only eleven and a half years apart. He's got anger problems like my mother and me. Don't take his kindness for weakness, and that's a warning from his sister. He doesn't take mess from nobody, and yes, he will tell you how he feels about any situation. Most people don't know, but that guy, my little brother Jay Edward, he's my best friend. And I wouldn't change him for anything in the world.

Maybe my bobble-head bubba did change me, for the better. Because now I have someone who looks up to me all the time. Someone who's on my every move at all times. I've always had someone to take care of, such as my grandparents and little cousins. That much hasn't changed. I've always been the helper. I love to take care of people, especially if I think they're in need and I care about them. To have someone depend on you means they trust you.

My attitude toward my brother changed for the good. Every day I think about what would have happened if I had never changed my thinking. My little brother would have grown to resent me when he got older. I know that I would have never been able to accept that. Having him depend on me is great, because I know everyone needs someone to depend on.

Seventeen-year-old **Unique Smith** is most inspired by her great-uncle, whose spirit was never broken, even after more than thirty years in prison. Unique considers herself outspoken, real, goofy, and moody. She enjoys doing hair, babysitting, being with friends, reading, and writing. Her goals include graduating from high school, going to college, and having a family of her own.

BEFORE I GOT
PREGNANT I ALWAYS
HEARD PARENTS
TELLING THEIR KIDS TO
FINISH HIGH SCHOOL,
GO TO COLLEGE, AND
MAKE A LIFE FOR
THEMSELVES. NOW I
CAN HONESTLY SAY I
UNDERSTAND WHY THEY
TOLD THEIR KIDS THAT.

The Unexpected Miracle
Courtney Hill

Parents are always telling their kids to finish high school, go to college, and make a life for themselves. Well, my senior year I didn't have any intentions of finishing high school. I just wanted to move on with my personal life and be on my own. I didn't want to worry about school anymore. I wanted freedom.

I was skipping school a lot more than I knew I should have. Eventually I stopped going to my classes. I had been getting involved with this one guy, John. Eventually all my time was spent being around him. I started to think that he was Mr. Wonderful, that nothing could go wrong between us. I thought I would spend the rest of my life with him.

After a month or so I began to notice some changes in my moods and how I was feeling. I just thought I was going through an emotional state. I had no idea a bigger situation was going to be on my hands.

I spent days trying to push aside the thought that there could be something seriously wrong with me. I began to throw up in the mornings. I had very abnormal cravings, like pickles with chocolate syrup on them and a pickle, peanut butter, and mayo sandwich. My stomach was getting hard, like I was bloated, kind of like a balloon. That is when I knew I needed to take a pregnancy test.

I didn't hesitate to take the test. I knew that I needed to know the truth about being pregnant and what I needed to do for my unborn child and myself. I went to the nearest drug store to pick up a test and the second I got home I ran to the bathroom and took it. I then waited the suggested time to make sure the test would come back as accurate as possible.

As I waited, I sat there wondering if I would have to change myself or if I could just stay very mysterious with myself like I had been used to being with my friends. That was the main thing rolling around in my mind. I also began to think, what would I do with this other human being? I could barely take care of myself.

While thinking, I saw the test was beginning to show a plus sign, which completely shocked me since I knew that meant I would be carrying around another human inside of my stomach for nine months. Then I would be responsible for taking care of this little person for the next eighteen years until it could go out into the world on its own. Now with all this on my mind, I was stressing over one major thing: How would I explain to John that "we" are having a baby?

Besides everything else, I knew that I would need to get in to see a doctor to learn exactly how far along I could be with my pregnancy. I made an appointment at the Maternity and Infant Care Clinic at the University of Washington Medical Center, When I went on June 30th, they asked a lot of questions, like when my last menstrual cycle was, how far along I thought I was, and when was the last time I had taken any drugs or alcohol. I answered all the questions truthfully, and the questions that I didn't know exact answers to I answered to the best of my knowledge.

The doctor told me I would need to take an ultrasound to figure out exactly how far along I was. I was excited to see what my baby would look like. But most importantly, I was nervous to find out how far along I was by then.

The doctor came back and told me I was four months into my pregnancy and that my expected due date was probably going to be around November 8th. I dropped my jaw. And I started to rethink how I could inform John.

I knew I also needed to do something for myself, and that was finishing school so I could lead a career of my own, rather than working at a McDonalds for the rest of my life and having to raise a child on minimum wage. Even though I had morning sickness, I had to manage to pull myself up out of bed to get the education I would need to make my life and my unborn child's life better for the future. I managed to take up some extra childbirth and parenting classes to help me in the future. I was on the right track.

As far as John, things seemed to get worse once I got up enough courage to tell him that "we" would have a baby. He kept telling me that "we" weren't ready to have a baby and that "we" weren't mature enough to take care of a baby. He made me think he was in denial of having a child at such a young age, and I began to think maybe I couldn't do this after all. But actually when I started to have these thoughts about not taking responsibility for something that I had created, and something that I had done to get into this situation, I went and pulled my grandma June aside and asked what she thought I should do and if I was wrong for having those thoughts.

We sat and talked about the entire situation that evening. She began to tell me that it was to be expected for a young teen, or in my case a young adult mother, to have those kind of feelings the first time around and that there was nothing that I should worry about. She kept telling me that if he really wanted to be with me that he would understand why I would want to have this child for my own, and that if he didn't understand, then he was not worth being with or even worth my time and effort, especially when he showed that he didn't even care about my feelings toward having "our" child.

I wasn't trying to push things to the side. But I thought the best thing, for both my unborn child and myself, was to just move on and do what I had to do, which was to focus on my child, myself, and school. But I really couldn't focus on that because I had John on my mind. I really didn't want to lose what John and I had, but he was bringing my spirits down for what I wanted to do, and that needed to be changed. So I decided to call John and have a talk with him.

"Hey baby," John answered the phone with excitement in his voice. I kind of hesitated to say, "Hello."

"Baby, are you okay? You sound like something is botherin' you," John said with a questioning tone in his voice.

"Well there is somethin' on my mind that I have been wantin' to talk to you about. Somethin' that is very serious and I think you really should be payin' attention to what I am 'bout to say," I said with a firm voice.

I was trying to make my tone as firm as possible to show John that I was having a very serious moment and not trying to joke around. Because John's a joker. He loves to be silly and joke around with people. I joke around with people too. But the topic of "us," John and me having a baby, isn't something to joke around with.

"Um…okay! Is there something I should be concerned about?" John asked in confusion.

"Okay no…. It really doesn't deal with me. Well yeah it does, but I didn't do anything for this to happen. Well yeah, actually I did and it involves you too," I said, trying not to confuse myself while telling him that I'm pregnant with his child and that I was keeping it.

"What? Has to deal with me? What did I do? You're not breaking up with me, are you? Please say that you aren't breaking it off," John asked, jumping to conclusions.

John was good at jumping to conclusions. That's why I always hesitate to talk to him, but then wasn't the time to hesitate. It was time to just be straightforward. No being shy, or telling John only half of the story. It was time for the entire story and the truth at that.

"No! Well, okay. Maybe it's going to be hard to explain this to you. Baby… I took a pregnancy test this morning and reassured myself that I was pregnant still. And yes, I am for sure pregnant with your child," I said, knowing that something wrong was about to happen.

"But now the thing is, are you going to stay with me? Even after I have our child?"

"Man! Are you serious?" John asked. I knew he was shocked as hell about having a child. I just didn't know what he would do now.

"Yes, baby, I'm serious," I said holding back tears.

"Man… this is something crazy," John said as he paced around the room while on the phone with me. "I need some time to myself to think about this before making a stupid decision and regretting it. I'll call you later."

John hung up. I sat there almost in tears with my cell phone in my hands. John just hung up without saying "goodbye" or "I love you." What am I going to do? Am I going to lose him forever or will things work out between us? These questions ran through my mind a lot after John hung up on me.

Several hours went by and still no call back from John. Thoughts of him cheating or doing something stupid like turning to drugs or drinking alcohol to wash away the "problem at hand" went through my mind. I didn't know what to do. Should I try to call him? Should I just leave him alone? I decided to just focus on my baby and me. I started to think of how I would get the money to get things that the baby needed, like a crib, stroller, car seat, clothes, diapers, wipes, and much more.

I started to realize that maybe I couldn't do these things, for babies cost a lot and I don't have a job; nor was I finished getting my high school diploma. How could I get the things babies require as well as giving it the love and care that it needs?

John did eventually call three days later. I answered. "Hello, John."

"Hey. I don't know if you even wanna talk to me. But I thought that I would call and tell what I have been thinking about rather than just let things sit where we are right now, which probably would be good for us," John said.

"What are you talking about?" I asked in confusion. " Are you tryin' to tell me that we should not go any farther with this relationship?"

"See, there you go again with jumpin' to conclusion 'bout things," he said to me with a firm, angry voice. "Why do you always do that?"

"I don't mean to. It is just you sound like it and that's why I said that."

"Well you need to stop asking questions to everything I say or when I ask you for something or for you to give me something. You shouldn't have to ask a bunch of questions just to see if I'm lyin' to you," he said.

"You make it seem like you don't do anything wrong anymore, John," I said with frustration.

"I don't do anything wrong. I tell you everything. What do I honestly have to hide from you anyways? I have absolutely nothing to hide from you," John said

"Okay. Whatever. You're right huh? You don't do nothing wrong. You're just Mr. Perfect," I said. "Ha. Yeah, right. That ain't true. I thought you were but you're not at all."

"Whatever, Courtney," he replied sounding annoyed. "Stop tryin' to flip things on to me."

"Okay, John, you know what? Why don't we just end things here because I can't do this no more with you," I stated firmly. "This is way too much to even be worrying about. I have more important things to be taking care of. Rather then you sitting here, just bringing me down more and more every day. So I'm done!"

I hung up the phone, not even giving him a chance to say anything back. I couldn't deal with the added stress anymore. I knew what I needed to do, and that was look forward to my new life with my child. I already was going to have a big responsibility taking care of one child; I wasn't in need of taking care of my child's father as if he was a child, too.

So I took the initiative to start making that life before my child came into this world. I was really focusing on trying to finish high school and get my diploma. Education was an important thing to me just because of the fact that I would be the first in my family to go on to college. I wanted more for my future with my child.

Days went by so fast after making my decision. I was getting closer and closer to my due date. I started to become more and more nervous as I realized that soon I would be in the hospital waiting to have my child.

I had many questions. What would happen to me? Would I be okay? Will anything hurt the baby? Will I end up staying in the hospital a long time or will I leave after a day? These questions were making me scared to have my child. That is when I decided to sit down again with my Grandma June.

My grandma was the only person I could trust talking to besides a doctor or a nurse. She knew a lot more than my own mother did, because she is a lot older and has had a lot more experience with things.

"Grandma, do you think that everything will be okay? Or do you think that something will go wrong and I'll have to stay in the hospital a long time?" I asked nervously. "That scares me!"

"For heaven sakes, child, nothing will happen to you. These are trained professional doctors and nurses. They have gone through a lot of school to get where they are. Plus, they won't let anything happen to a baby," my grandma told me.

"Okay. I hope not…but what happens if I lose too much blood?" I asked, scared out of my mind.

"They know what to do with that, too," my grandma replied with a smile. "Courtney Marie, everything will be okay. Plus, I'm going to be right there with you."

"Okay. I'm trusting you," I replied.

My grandma June was like a mother figure to me. When my mother couldn't be around because of going to work or to college, my grandma was right there helping me grow and learn. I love her for that. If it weren't for my grandma being around for my pregnancy, I would have been a total mess. Not knowing what to do. Being terrified about what would happen.

Days went by. Now I had exactly twenty-four hours before I'd go into the hospital to have my child. I was nervous, but I was excited to finally hold my child in my arms and have my child in my life.

I sat there on my bed with my cell phone right in front of me waiting to see if I would get a phone call from John. I didn't get one. I wish that I had, but I wasn't going to weaken myself by calling him to say that I hope he hopes that everything is going to be okay with his child and me.

I started to get things together for my stay at the hospital. I packed all the baby clothes I thought I would need, together with newborn diapers and wipes. Then I made sure that I had the baby's car seat by the front door ready to be picked up and taken to the hospital.

Then it was time to pack for myself. I wasn't completely sure what I would need, so I just decided to take the most comfortable clothes that I had, my slippers for when I would walk around and books so I could read while waiting. I also packed some movies for my grandma to watch while she was there waiting with me. November 1, 2006, was here and I was in the waiting room. My heart was beating rapidly. I didn't know what would happen next. It was around 9:15 a.m. before the nurse came in to tell me that I was able to go back to my room to start the long, or possibly short, process of delivering my child. I went to my room and the nurse gave me a gown.

While I went into the bathroom and changed, my grandma June sat in the other room watching the television.

After I changed, the nurse came back in to start me on the medication to speed up labor. The nurse inserted my IV, so that she could start the Pitocin and the hydration fluid. I sat there as the nurse poked the needle into the skin of my hand, thinking about whether my child would have to have an IV or a feeding tube. Would things be okay, so it wouldn't have to be monitored, or would it have to be put in the ICU? Those were all things that I was worried about. But I really tried hard to not let them bother me.

The nurse said she would start my induction. I just sat on the side of my hospital bed and said to myself that I needed to be calm and that I needed to think positive thoughts. I knew that if I stayed calm things would completely okay with both my child and me.

Several hours passed but nothing progressed. My labor wasn't as bad as I thought it would have been by then. I was having contractions, though, and they hurt badly. I was sitting there thinking I really wasn't wanting to have a C-section, but I knew that was going to happen anyway, because eight hours had gone by and my child wasn't dropping into the birth canal at all. I dreaded having a C-section. I was even more nervous than when I first got to the hospital.

Around two o'clock in the morning a doctor came into my room and checked how things were and then told me that I was in need of having a C-section. The nurse told me to get as much rest as I could. It was November 2, 2006. The nurse gathered everything that was needed for my operation and rolled my hospital bed into the operating room, then went back to the other room and got my grandma June.

I was terrified. I didn't want to go through with having surgery. But I knew that it was all for a good reason, to have my child come into the world. I just wanted the entire operation to be over, so I could have my child in my arms.

Everything in the operating room seemed to go very fast. Within minutes the doctor started the operation and I had my child. That's when I found out that the baby was a boy. He was born at 8:59 in the morning. I was thrilled that I had my son in this world finally.

I had decided that I would name him Daymein James. Daymein was a name that I liked and James was to be after my father and John's grandfather, who I never knew but heard lots of interesting things about. And I thought that it would be a blessing to name my son after him and my own father.

When I heard his first cry I looked at my grandma June. We were so happy that we both had tears in our eyes. Then the nurse brought him over so I could see him. I wanted to cry tears of joy because I was shocked that this little human was growing inside of my body. After they had finished cleaning him up, they brought him to my grandma and she held him while the doctors finished stitching me up.

Having a baby has taught me a lot. From now on my life will be filled with lots of changes for both my child and me. I'm truly blessed that I have Daymein in my life and that he has changed my life for the better.

Before I got pregnant I always heard parents telling their kids to finish high school, go to college, and make a life for themselves. Now I can honestly say I understand why they told their kids that. There could come a day where they could have kids of their own, and the parents just want what is best for both their child and their grandchild. Having parents give their kids encouraging advice helps change their future for the better. Do you think your life would be better with a change? Answer this for yourself, and see the outcome.

Despite the concentration it took to finish her story, and the frustration she felt
as she was writing it, twenty-one-year-
old **Courtney Hill** loved this book project. Now she's focused on finishing high
school, going to college, and becoming
a medical assistant. She is inspired by
her son and by other single mothers
who "struggle like me."

BUT THIS WAR WAS
NOT TAKING PLACE
IN VIETNAM. IT WAS
TAKING PLACE IN
SEATTLE. THE YEAR
WAS 1964.

What If...
Douglas Ho

What if... it happened here? What if the setting changed? Once upon a time the leader of North Vietnam, Ho Chi Minh, and five hundred North Vietnamese gangsters were at war over money with the leader of South Vietnam, Nguyen Van Thieu, and one hundred South Vietnamese. The North was trying to take the South's money because the South was making fifty million dollars more than the North. This made the North angry because they wanted to be richer than the South, so the North began moving into the South's territory by plane to take their money.

But this war was not taking place in Vietnam. It was taking place in Seattle. The year was 1964. Seattle was divided into North and South by the REI store. The South decided that the REI was going to separate North and South.

How did the South beat the North?

While still in Vietnam, the South ran behind and on top of buildings. Thirty of the South were guarding fifty million dollars. They had the best weapons in the world because they spent the most money on them, and they got the weapons from China. They spent twenty-three million dollars on the guns and bombs.

Nguyen Van Thieu got on his private jet and headed to Seattle. The mob from the North followed him. When Nguyen got off the plane, the North started shooting, and Nguyen's army helped him. They shot back at the North and brought the leader of the South inside. The South Vietnamese kept shooting the North Vietnamese. The North fired back.

Nguyen called up his brother in Vietnam, who got on a jet with a big bomb. He flew to Seattle and dropped the bomb on the North. The North died. The South won.

Ho Chi Minh showed up in Seattle. Nguyen came out of the building loaded up with a whole bunch of weapons and ran to take cover to find Ho Chi Minh. Ho Chi Minh was walking around looking for Nguyen, so the rest of the South army all gathered up behind the Space Needle. Then they all ran in after Ho Chi Minh and started shooting him from the back.

Ho Chi Minh stayed alive even when he had fifty bullets in him. Then he spotted the leader of the South and shot him two times in the leg. After that, Nguyen started running. He turned around and shot Ho Chi Minh right in the middle of the head. Ho Chi Minh died.

There was only one more survivor from the North. The survivor ran to Ho Chi Minh's jet and flew back to the North Vietnam to get more soldiers from the North. The captain of the North then recruited more people from the North for a meeting. The captain recruited seven hundred people. The captain went to the phone and called up China to buy weapons.

Meanwhile, in the South, out of the hundred people, thirty-two died, eighteen were injured, and the other fifty were safe.

The South kept the money.

TO BE CONTINUED...

"Fast, funny, and loud" is how thirteen-year-old **Douglas Ho** describes himself. He loves playing basketball, and he hopes to attend college. What does he like most about himself? "Anything."

I DON'T THINK I HAVE AS
MUCH ANGER AS I HAD
BEFORE. I THINK I JUST
HAD THE ANGER FOR
A WHILE BUT IT WENT
AWAY. I HAVE CHANGED
THE WAY I ACT BE-
CAUSE OF MY SCHOOL.

Changes
Vanessa Quiroz

Two years ago, in sixth grade, I had a lot of anger. I lived in Moses Lake and I went to Chief Moses Middle School. I had a best friend. Her name was Karina. We had known each other for three years and we got into a lot of arguments. That's where some of my anger came from, but during the arguments we never broke our friendship apart because we always ended up talking things out.

One day I was talking to a guy named Josh. All of the girls liked him, even my best friend. But he liked me and she didn't know that. No one told her and I kind of didn't want her to know because I knew she would get mad at me. Then he asked me why I liked to hang out with Karina and I told him not to worry about it. That day, I walked up to Karina to say hi, but she walked away and I could tell that she was mad at me. So I walked back up to her and asked her if she was mad and she said yes.

I asked why and she said because Josh told her something that wasn't true. She believed him. I was very mad, so I didn't talk to her for a while. She came up to me and asked if I was talking about her.

I said, "No, why would I?"

She said, "Well, I heard from Josh that you said you didn't like to hang out with me."

I said, "No, I never said that."

She didn't believe me because she liked Josh and wanted to believe him and not me. I was very mad. After I heard that Josh said that and lied to her about what I said, I didn't ever talk to him again. The next day I was with some other friends. I guess she got mad because I wasn't showing her any attention. So when it was time to switch periods, I went to my next class, and she tried to trip me. I got mad and we started to fight and hit each other. I got expelled because it was my fourth time fighting at that school.

The day after that, my mom decided to move to Seattle. She had gotten tired of living in a small town. My sister, on the other hand, didn't want to move because she said she didn't feel like it, so she stayed in Moses Lake. My mom, stepdad, little brother, and I went. When we got there we lived with my aunt for a couple of months. While we were living there, my mom was trying to get me to go back to school, but no school would accept me because of the problems that I got into at Moses Lake. So I didn't go school for the rest of the year.

Now I'm going to school and I haven't gotten into any fights. I don't think I have as much anger as I had before. I think I just had the anger for a while but it went away. I have changed the way I act because of my school. I like the different students. The teachers don't have many rules. They're less strict. In Seattle, they let me do more stuff. For example, at my old school in Moses Lake, they wouldn't let us eat in the rooms and we would have to raise a hand just to get out of our seats. Over here, where I go to school, we don't have to raise a hand and we can eat in the rooms. We have more choices.

So these problems helped me in my life to be a better person and not to fight. And now I'm doing fine, not fighting or getting involved with the police or anything like that.

Fourteen-year-old **Vanessa Quiroz** plans to become a nurse after finishing high school. She enjoys playing basketball and is inspired by her grandmother and mother. This is her first time being published.

MY UNCLE USED TO TELL
ME THAT PEOPLE WERE
PREJUDICED TOWARD
BLACKS, BUT I DIDN'T
REALLY BELIEVE HIM
UNTIL I SAW IT FOR
MYSELF... I'M GLAD I'M
NOT PREJUDICED TOWARD
OTHERS, BECAUSE
THAT'S NOT RIGHT.

Is It Worth It?
DeAndre Eaton

Change can mean different things to different people. I feel I can change some things, but other things I can't change at all. Having a new house is one of the things I could change. I want to have my own home, because my mom won't let me do half the things I want to. I want to be able to stay up until after 10:00 p.m. on school nights, watch television, and play video games. I want to be able to walk on the carpet with my shoes on. If I walk on the carpet now, my mom gets mad, because she wants to keep it clean. Sometimes, she even makes me clean it with carpet cleaner. So, that's why I would like to have my own house, and it could happen someday.

But I can't change gangs and drugs and guns, even though I wish I could. Gangs are things people need to change. People die over gangs, and that's not the way to go. Gangsters shoot each other, and they shoot innocent people. There goes another person dead, for no reason.

Drugs need to stop, too. People sell drugs, people get put in prison over drugs, and sometimes people get shot over drugs. There goes another person dead, and that's not the way to go.

I knew of someone who got hurt because he was dealing drugs and sold bad crack to a crack-head, who pulled out a gun and shot him. I heard of another guy who got shot, because he beat up a local gang member. The gangster remembered his face, and twenty minutes later came back, pulled out a gun, and shot the guy in the leg. He lived to tell the story.

If I could, I would even go back in time and try to change slavery. Some people are still scared of black people today, just like they were back then. I don't like it when people prejudge me because I am black, or think they know me. They really don't know anything about me. I think they are just scared, and that's not right. I would love to change that.

My uncle used to tell me that people were prejudiced toward blacks, but I didn't really believe him until I saw it for myself. I was with my friend and we were playing football with other friends and people they knew. When they decided to choose teams, I didn't get picked. They said they didn't have room, but there was room for three more players, so I knew it was because I was black. As I was watching them play, I really wished that I was playing, too, but that is just how life is. It felt like no one wanted me on the team, that no one in the world wanted me. I'm glad I'm not prejudiced toward others, because that's not right.

I'm so glad that I'm not in a gang and I don't do any drugs, because it's not safe. It's not worth it. People do drugs, and they do stupid things. People join gangs for protection, then get shot at or killed. (I wonder if gang members visit their homies in the hospital when they get shot, or in prison when they shoot others?)

Maybe if people stayed out of gangs, stopped doing drugs, and stayed in school, everybody would be fine. Because, it's not guns that kill people, it's stupid people with guns that kill people.

How does thirteen-year-old **DeAndre Eaton** feel about this book project? "I think it's cool that someone believes in John Marshall kids." As one of those students, DeAndre hopes to succeed in school, change his anger, and eventually become a professional athlete. His hobbies include football, baseball, basketball, soccer, and chess.

I WOKE UP ON A GURNEY
ON THE STAIRS AT
MY DAD'S APARTMENT
AND ASKED, "WHAT
HAPPENED?" I ONLY
REMEMBERED FALLING
ASLEEP ON THE COUCH
WITH A HEADACHE.

Fall in Life
Jessica Hoyt

I had a seizure seven months ago and almost died.

I woke up on a gurney on the stairs at my dad's apartment and asked, "What happened?" I only remembered falling asleep on the couch with a headache.

"We don't know," the paramedics answered. "All we know is something is wrong."

I could tell they were worried because their squinting eyes looked concerned. I felt very upset and scared. I felt a lot of pain in my tongue, which I later found was from where I bit it during the seizure.

The paramedics took me to the hospital in Bremerton. They kept me there for four hours until they realized that my condition was more serious than they thought. Since they didn't have a brain center, they took me to the Mary Bridge Children's Hospital in Tacoma, where they have a terrific brain center.

When I got to the Mary Bridge Children's Hospital, they started doing tests. They wheeled me into a room with a big, gray metal tube called an MRI machine. They put me in the tube, a sort of x-ray device, so they could look at my brain.

I stayed in my hospital room for three long days. I was both very bored and very scared. Everything was new and strange to me, especially at night. The beeping heart and IV monitors kept waking me up at night. They put these things on my head, called an EEG. During the day, I watched TV, played video games, and ate a lot of pudding. The doctors woke me up early each morning to give me pills. After I took my pills, I had to order all of my meals, which seemed odd because I wasn't used to having so many choices.

The only good part about this was that all my friends and family came and visited. I got a ton of attention and a lot of gifts.

Then, on top of all that, my sister and I had to move away from our dad. We moved from Bremerton to Oak Harbor to live with our mom. We didn't go to school for a couple months because we knew that we were going to have to move again soon. Our mom didn't want us too get used to it, to make friends and then have to leave again.

We eventually did move again, this time to Seattle. We started school a few weeks after we got here. I'm going to the best school I've ever been to, called John Marshall Alternative School.

I had a seizure seven months ago and almost died. There has been a lot of change in my life since then.

I wake up in a room I share with my sister at my mom's house, filled with posters. I used to have my own room but now we are squeezed in tight in a one-bedroom apartment.

I've met a lot of new people since we moved, but I miss all of my friends in Bremerton.

I don't get to hang out or do anything without my sister or my mom because I have to be with someone who knows what to do when I have a seizure. My mom is scared that I am going to have a seizure and no one will be there to help me. This is a big change because I used to be way more independent and hang out with my friends at the mall. My mom is also scared that I might do something I'm not supposed to do.

I have a health problem that I have to live with for the rest of my life. I'm taking a lot of pills for my seizures and headaches. I have to go to a lot of doctor appointments in Tacoma and it takes a long time to get over there.

This experience has changed how I have to lead my life, but it hasn't changed who I am.

Fifteen-year-old **Jessica Hoyt** considers herself funny, weird, and lovable, and considers fellow John Marshall author Breanna Alexander an inspiration. She loves to swim and sing, and hopes one day to become a professional singer. What are her thoughts about this book project? "Really cool."

USUALLY THE WORD
"SURE" SHOULD BE
DIRECTED TOWARD
SOMETHING YOU'D
ENJOY DOING,
SOMETHING THAT
WOULDN'T CAUSE YOU
TEARS OR ANY SORT OF
PAIN. AT LEAST THAT'S
WHAT I BELIEVED.

Sure Doesn't Always Mean Yes
(Exaggerated, but Somewhat True)
Christine Leslie

"Sure."

Let's take one swift moment to think on the word "sure." "Sure, I'll have some ice cream." "Sure, I'd like to go swimming." Usually the word "sure" should be directed toward something you'd enjoy doing, something that wouldn't cause you tears or any sort of pain. At least that's what I believed. Oh, how severely wrong I was.

"Sure, let's move to Washington."

It really shouldn't be that simple. Hell, the word "sure" shouldn't even exist! I am now deciding to erase that wicked word from all existence. Now, I bet you are wondering what's up with my intense hate toward a simple word. Well, first off that word was the reason, the number one reason for my move, the terrible, vile move from a little resort town called Lake Havasu, Arizona, to the big city of Seattle.

I distinctly remember that move. I remember my surroundings, my feelings, everything. That's proof enough that the move made an impact on my life, but was moving a good idea? Not even remotely.

It was my mother who asked me to move up to Seattle. She just randomly brought it up, out of the blue. It was as if she planned to ambush me. But I remember the look in her eyes was so distraught, begging almost, as she spoke. "Honey, will you move to Washington with me?" How could I deny my mother? It wasn't even fair of her to ask me. I mean, she's my mother. I loved her and my love ran deep, even though she did screw her life over. I felt that it'd be betrayal if I remained. What other choice did I have?

And so I said sure. After everything that happened I couldn't just allow my mother, my beloved mother, to be alone. And, oh, the things that happened! Get a director over here, stat, we've got a movie to make! But in all seriousness, the things that happened should never have come to pass. Even today, three years later, I still wish I'd never said yes to her question.

At that moment in time the idea Mom presented sounded simply delicious. "Get away, Melissa, just get away." That's what I thought after the initial shock of the question wore off. But then, as days passed by, I thought of everything I'd lose. My friends, my family, my dearly loved dog, everything. I began having second thoughts about that sure.

Each time the thought of talking to my mother came up I'd think, "No, that's not a good idea. Your mother needs you, and you need to get out of here." And I loved my mother; I loved her with all my heart. I wanted to be with her, so instead of allowing those thoughts I'd think back on my life in Arizona. I ran through the ghastly things that happened.

Sarah, my mother, had been into drugs for years. It never really bothered me, but there were times when I hated her. I hated her with all my heart for choosing drugs over me. I knew the drugs had chained her to the floor.

I hated the fact that I didn't know my father. I mean I knew him from our phone conversations but I didn't know him. And I knew, should we move to Washington, I would get to know this man whom

I had never met. See, I used to live in Washington with him and my mother when I was two, but at that age you can't really know anybody. To me his face was a dull blur, his personality—all my creation.

Even to this day I remember their fighting, and I remember Sarah being pulled away in a cop car because of said fighting. That was the last time I ever saw my father, and I guess I should have hated him more; he could have come to see me, after all, but he never did. Every time he'd call me, he'd be in jail or just getting out. I was young, I thought, maybe this time he'll stay out of jail. Maybe this time he'll stay drug free, for me. I was so childish.

My grandmother, the woman I called Granny and barely knew as Crystal, was like a second mother to me. Not only did she care for me while my mother was in and out of jail for her various drug charges, but she also cared for my sister, Erica. I knew that we were hard work, me throwing my constant tantrums and Erica getting into cigarettes, weed, and fights. Even though I knew that, seeing my sister being hit by Granny sent anger all through my body. I think I screamed at Granny, but I can't be sure. Even though she did that, and many other incredibly horrid things, I still loved the old woman. If I moved she'd be something I'd lose.

Sarah screwed up big time once. She'd found herself a man online, Brett Steel. Oh, I liked him, at first, but I didn't see through his façade. After a few months of having a long-distance relationship with Brett, she decided to move in with him. And off we went to Tucson. It was great! I had friends; I had a tremendous school that I could walk to; I had money (this guy was freaking rich). But they fought, they fought like mad dogs and I barely even noticed it! I was still too young to realize what was going on, but what's worse is that Sarah allowed it. She allowed this man to hit her, thinking she loved him. She let it go on for months until this guy hit Erica. After that it was over. Sarah'd never allow anybody to hurt her children. Mom, bleeding because Brett had hit her with a phone, told him to get out. She called the cops and eventually they got him. Know how long he got? Like two months! But they added other charges, like parole violation. All in all he got about two years, but he died not long ago. Karma's a wicked woman, isn't she?

Sarah may have loved Brett for that short amount of time, but her true love was always Leonard. Leonard was a tall man with a belly that looked like he was pregnant (it was hilarious to tease the man). He was a friend of my uncle since childhood, and God only knows if they were together before the big guy got sent to prison. It wasn't long after we moved back to Havasu that Leonard got out, and it felt like an instant hookup to me. We all lived together for a while, at Granny's, but Mom and Granny fought like cats and dogs. I distinctly remember having many, many dishes broken in fits of rage. So our little family decided to split up from Granny and get our own home.

Still I was hidden away from the drugs my mother and Leonard did. However, everything changed when we got our own place. I suddenly realized that there was something going on, or maybe I just grew up, but either way I knew. I knew that they were screwing themselves over; I knew that eventually something bad would ensue and then what would happen to Erica and me? I used to blame a lot of it on Leonard, thinking it was all his fault that the drugs were entering our house, but once again I was blind to the truth. Even if Leonard hadn't been there, Mom would have found a way to get her poison.

Yeah, I liked that little place we got. In fact, I adored it! It was connected to two other houses, both of which contained people that would become my family. But we would soon move from that place as well, though I can't remember why exactly. Maybe I never knew. We moved from place to place, new apartments, a hotel (which sucked completely, by the way), and also to Leonard's mom's house. We finally got a little apartment with Leonard, and the fights followed. I heard fights about drugs, about women that'd he'd get with, about things that I'd wished I'd never heard. It didn't take long for him to be kicked out, and that's when the pain really began.

When I heard the news, I don't think I believed it. "He murdered somebody," I heard. "He's on the run, they haven't found him." I didn't cry; I was amazed. Amazed that this man whom I had known since birth, whom I shared secrets and even allowed to be considered my father could kill someone. It wasn't plausible! We were mad, of course, my little family and I. How could he do this to us? And I'm not being selfish. People knew Leonard, knew he was with Sarah, and knew that

I was considered his kid. The cops even ambushed my mom once, raided our house while I watched through the peephole next door.

He was on the run for a while. I thought they'd never catch him, maybe I even hoped they wouldn't. But he strolled into a police office and turned himself in and the big murder case was kaput. He got twenty-something years, pretty much life. It took some time for us to get the facts, but when we did I learned a lesson. The reason he killed someone was because of drugs, and he was high at the time.

That should have been the end of our problems; really, did we need any more crap? Hell no! Not long after that Mom got sent to prison for three months and left my sister with custody of me. Mom's fellow drugs friends—James, Jim, and Jason—took care of us. I never really liked Jim that much, his tallness and ugliness irked me to no end, and I barely knew Jason, but James was like my uncle. Jim joined us in the apartment, along with my sister's best friend Lisa. Jim and Erica were spending time together, more time than was healthy. She was eighteen and he was like…thirty-six. Can we take a moment to exclaim how disgusting that is?

Lisa and I both confronted Erica about her relationship with Jim. "He's like my brother!" she swore. "I don't like him." To think I fell for the lies. It wasn't long before the wicked spider weaved his web around my sister. She became a tweaker, just like him. I didn't believe it. Even when her friends came and started yelling at her for tweaking, for being a hypocrite. I stood up for her.

"No, she's not! She'd never do that!" I screamed at those people, hating them for saying those horrible things.

It wasn't until later that I found out it was true. My sister had joined in with the druggies. I hated her for it. And for lying. And then, because Jim was such a jerk and a thief, my sister was arrested. The cops found stolen material in our apartment. I was sent to live with Granny again. When I went to go get my things from the house…oh, it was horrible. It was like walking into a tornado-torn house. The cops had gone through everything, torn things apart, and ruined almost the whole lot. It sent tears coursing down my face.

Almost as soon as my mom got out on parole she left, unable to pay the authorities the money they wanted. Off she ran to Las Vegas, now wanted in Lake Havasu. I missed her, but I was used to being without her. It was like she was in prison again. My sister stayed with Jim in some trailer home, and I didn't care about that either. I was still angry with her. My life continued on, somewhat peaceful as I lived with my Granny. That is until Mom decided to come pay a visit. And that's when I was presented with that challenging, horrible, and unfair question.

"Will you move to Washington with me?"

"Sure."

There was nothing else to say. I had to go. I couldn't change my mind, no matter what happened, no matter who I'd miss. I had to stay with my mother. But it was still unbearable saying good-bye to Katerina, the girl who became one of the most important people in my life, pretty much my sister. I cried at school, as did many of my friends. People I barely knew were coming up to me, telling me how it'd be totally different without me around, and I wanted to say, "Yeah, okay! I'll just stay!" But I couldn't do that. I had to move.

The plane ride was painful. I watched the state I grew up in slowly disappear from view, watched as everything I knew faded away. I was in complete jitters when I got off the plane, knowing the man I never really knew was soon going to enter my life. I thought it'd be a completely different meeting, but by then I'd started hating him for giving Sarah the option of coming up here. So the only thing I thought when I saw my father was, "Wow, I'm glad I don't look like that."

It wasn't a very good way to start out my new life. It wasn't like one of those Lifetime movies where the daughter would scream, "Daddy!" and run into the father's arms in tears. Oh no, it was much more awkward than that. In fact, until I moved up here and met the guy, I called him Dad, but then I thought, Is he really my dad? Leonard was more of a dad than this guy was. And so I decided he would never be known as Dad in my vocabulary. From then on I called him by his name. Lester.

Distraught. The word barely even covered the emotion I felt living up here. It was everything I hated about a city—cold, gray, lifeless. I grew angry that there was no dirt, I craved the sun, I spit at the green color that surrounded me. At night I would cry, wishing that somehow my mother would decide to turn back and serve her time for ditching parole. It never happened.

Time passed and my anger dimmed; I made new friends and a whole new life. I even tried to forget the pain that sat boldly in my past. It took me a while to realize that you couldn't just forget your past; it would always be there, haunting you until you accepted it. But I didn't want to accept it. I wanted to go back in time and try to fix things, and for a long while I was depressed, sleeping and eating more than was normal.

It was about a year later when something horrid happened, perhaps more horrid than all the other things that had occurred in my life. Erica had remained in Havasu with Jim to have a kid, my nephew, Chase. I loved him, though I wasn't able to meet him. When Sarah woke me that morning and told me he'd died in the night I didn't believe her. What a cruel joke, I thought. He's only three months old, of course he's not dead! But I was wrong. Chase was gone and I'd never be able to meet him.

When reality set in that my little nephew had really left this world for the next, I realized that I needed to get over the past; I couldn't allow myself to lose to my memories. And friends surrounded me. As tears slid down my cheeks my friends remained close to me, telling me that everything would be all right. I loved them for it. But still, I missed Katerina.

The wound of her being gone remained in my heart, and I believe it will always remain until I am able to see her again, but the true change happened when I met one of the most important people in my life. Xenia. When I met her many things in my life changed. The wounds that Katerina left in my heart became a mere scar. Xenia changed me from being the quiet homebody into a more outspoken person. It's as if when she arrived I received a personality. In fact, and I admit this quite willingly, meeting her was the only good thing that has ever happened to me up here. Sure I loved the friends I made, but I could live without them. I could, and it does hurt to say so.

Even so, I still wish I never had moved up here, I still wish I hadn't had to utter that word, sure. Why would I say that when I loved Xenia so? Why desire Havasu when it has so many bad memories? Well I believe that if we were meant to meet each other—even if I remained in Havasu—we would have. I know I won't be going back there, no matter how much I wish it. I know that I will remain here, in this gray city, with Xenia at my side. And I know that I will continue to change, for better or for worse, but no matter what I will always hold a piece of Havasu close to my scarred heart.

One of fifteen-year-old **Christine Leslie**'s goals is "to be stronger than the others." Christine would describe herself as odd, different, and not of this world. She appreciates her motherliness and enjoys sleeping, writing, reading, and eating. She is inspired by writers, notably David Clement Davies and J.R.R. Tolkien.

HE HAD HEARD OF
AMERICA ON TV AND
IN STORIES, AND HE
THOUGHT IT MUST BE
TOO GOOD TO BE TRUE,
A PLACE WHERE THERE
WERE LOTS OF JOBS
AND BIG CITIES AND
WHERE EVERYONE HAD
LOTS OF MONEY.

Running from Death
Saffia Harb Elhuraibi

My father is the greatest man I have ever met. He is a 46-year-old Arab man who came to the United States as a refugee. He is now a permanent resident and one day hopes to become an American citizen. He came to this country with a great story to tell, and I am going to tell it for him.

My father's name is Harb Elhuraibi. Before coming to the U.S., he lived in Ethiopia most of his life. During that time, many students wanted to overthrow the king, but the communists overthrew him instead and took power. The students did not want this to happen, because they believed the communists would take away their homes, farms, and freedom.

My father told me that many people who opposed the communists were killed, and that those who followed the communists were given guns. They used their guns to come to the schools and kill the students they had problems with. They would even go into mosques and kill people while they prayed.

The communists took two of my family's buildings and one mango farm. My father was only fifteen years old when this was going on and he was a student, so he was a target for murder. Because his mother, Saffia, was worried about his safety, she sold some of her gold to buy him a plane ticket to Yemen. She chose Yemen because that is where my father's family was from originally. My father stayed in Yemen for four months, returned to Africa and lived in Djibouti for a year, then moved to Saudi Arabia to work.

My father had been in Saudi Arabia a year when he changed countries again, this time to the United States. He had saved lots of money selling gold to people in Saudi Arabia, so he was able to make the move. He had heard of America on TV and in stories, and he thought it must be too good to be true, a place where there were lots of jobs and big cities and where everyone had lots of money. My dad thought it was a good idea to come to this great country, because he could work and become rich. He was young and wanted this opportunity to have a nice life.

When the communists took over Ethiopia, my father had to grow up quickly to keep himself safe. But in America, he could have a normal life, without running from death. His older brother, my uncle Mohamed, had come here many years earlier and had even fought as a U.S. Marine. My uncle was working for the Ford Motor Company when my dad arrived in the United States. My uncle had to move around a lot for his work, so my dad followed him from place to place. In California, my dad worked as a mailman and saved up lots of money, then moved to Minnesota, again to be with his brother. My dad liked the place, so he stayed for a very long time.

My dad told me that one day, while he was still in Minnesota, he walked into a restaurant and saw a beautiful Native American woman. He just had to talk to her! After only a few weeks, he and the woman (Dorothy) fell in love. They got married and within a few years, Dorothy became pregnant. On December 15, 1992, Dorothy had a beautiful baby girl, and they named her Saffia. That beautiful baby girl was me, Saffia Harb Elhuraibi. My father says that, because I was his first-born, I was automatically his princess. It was one of the happiest days of his life.

"I am really thankful that 826 Seattle gave me a chance to tell my father's story," says fourteen-year-old **Saffia Harb Elhuraibi**. Her father is one of her inspirations, because of the obstacles he has overcome. She says she's also inspired by her older sister, the quartet Ida, and supermodels Janice Dickinson and Tyra Banks. In fact, one of Saffia's goals is to be a supermodel herself, though she would also like to open an orphanage in Kenya and become a marine biologist. What does she like most about herself? "I am a very driven person, and I will accomplish my dreams!"

EVERYTHING USED TO
BE SO PERFECT, OR AT
LEAST IT WAS PERFECT
TO ME.

The "Cold, Cold" Summer
Jonishia Price

When I used to live in Federal Way, I had lots of fun. My friends and I always used to hang out at the basketball court (where all the boys were) and we used to play basketball. Personally, I think that basketball is very dumb and I do not like it at all, because I can't play it at all. The last time I played basketball I ended up tripping over the ball and fell on my face, and my eye was swollen. Me and my friends used to go swimming together almost every day. We went to the mall and everything, and we used to have so much fun. Everything used to be so perfect, or at least it was perfect to me, because I liked the way I lived and everything I was able to do when I was there. Now everything has changed ever since I have been in Seattle.

We decided to move back out to Seattle because we wanted to be closer to my grandmother. I thought it was a good idea too. Now we have been living here for about two and half years. When we were getting enrolled in school I was supposed to o to Aki Kurose because it was walking distance from my house. That school was full so I went to Meany Middle School. At first I thought it was a good school; it wasn't as bad as I thought it would be and I got along with a lot of people. I'd thought it was going to be some type of private school or something, and I think that private schools are bad because they are not out in the open. Not that I am racist or anything, but I like to be around a lot of black people, and I thought that school was going to be full of white people. It turned out to be more blacks than whites, but there was this girl there who just didn't like me for whatever reason.

The next school year came around and I was in the eighth grade, all my friends and me. That girl still didn't like me. I didn't care, but then rumors started going around the school that she liked my boyfriend. I really didn't understand that because she had a boyfriend, but she just wanted to mess with mine.

Then I got into trouble for skipping school with my boyfriend and his friend. We weren't even gone for that long, but when we came back my boyfriend and I got caught and his friend was saved (didn't anybody know that he had left). My boyfriend and I ended up going to John Marshall Alternative School.

One Friday after school I went to my cousin Naenae's house and spent the night. On Saturday I caught the bus home and on the way I saw this other girl that went to Meany with me, and now she went to Marshall with me, too. Her name is Summer. We were homies. I can say that we were homies because we always used to hang out with each other and we did things together and we used to talk. I took her back when she was about to get into a fight with another female I knew. I thought Summer was a good friend.

When we got on the bus, there was the other girl that went to Meany that had a problem with me, with some other females. Summer and I went to the back of the bus, but those girls came to the back with us. The girl that didn't like me was back there just saying stupid stuff like, "I don't like you because I think you are ugly," and

"I don't like you because you took the boy I wanted to go out with." She was talking about the boy that I was going out with at the time named Victor. Then it was finally time for me to get off the bus, and as I was leaving I heard them talking in the back of the bus saying, "If you don't like her you need to fight her."

As I walked home I heard them behind me. Summer had called my name, then I turned around and started to take off my backpack, ready to fight, when one of the girls stopped me and said, "What are you taking your backpack off for? She don't want to fight you, she just wants to talk to you." I stopped and we talked for about five minutes, then I told them that I had to go because I was like two hours late getting home. So as I was walking they were following me, and I just knew if they were still following me by the time I had made it into my house that all of my cousins and sisters would come out and it would be going down, but we stopped by a school that is right by my house. They were saying, "Jonishia, you have to fight her right now or else when you see her on the streets you will have to fight her and her family may be with her." I was thinking for a minute and then I was like, "I am not stupid enough to fight her right here and end up getting jumped by all of you."

All of a sudden, Summer turned against me. She knew if we were to fight then they would win because there were all of them against me. Summer tried to spray mace in my eyes and I caught her. I knew from that point forward not to trust anybody even if they are a friend. I was getting so mad and I couldn't wait until I saw her at school.

When I went back to school Monday, Summer was not there. On Tuesday I was absent, but on Wednesday we both were there. I approached her while she was arguing with Victor and when she was done I called her out. Evidently she was scared because she went back inside of the classroom and was like, "Jonishia, I don't want to fight you, you're a little kid." The bell rang and I went to class.

At lunchtime my sister came up to me and told me to follow her. As we left the lunchroom we saw Summer at the top of the hallway and when she saw us she started to run toward the office. Next thing I knew my sister was running after her and I was running after my sister. When we reached the office my sister asked Summer, "You want to jump my sister when you have four other people with you, but when she wants to fight you one-on-one you want to run away?"

Summer started to get loud with my sister and my sister was ready to fight her and I had to push my sister out of the way because she was pregnant and I didn't want her fighting. I called Summer out to fight me again and since it was lunchtime everyone was starting to gather around us. Then the security came and Summer started to drop her coat and stuff so I tried to break through the security and get her and that didn't work either. My sister tried to go to the other office door to get in but they had locked it. I was so mad!

So the principal came and said that if we try to fight Summer during school, coming to school, or leaving school that we could go to juvenile and that they didn't think that we'd want to be there with the holiday coming up. I knew I didn't want to be there for Christmas. I was about to be getting presents from everyone, and I was not about to fight her and ruin it for myself. But I knew if I saw her on the streets or somewhere else I would be forced to fight her. She'd really made me mad the way she just turned on me that day, how she was just talking with me and giggling with me like twenty minutes before all this started on that bus. I really don't feel that anyone has ever made me as mad as she did, cause I was mad about that for hella long.

Since our fallout, I have seen her so many times in school but didn't fight her because I just figured it was a waste of my time. Besides, I knew she didn't want to fight me anyway, because she ran the first two times. One day she even had the audacity to talk to her friends about what had happened; except she told them that I had run from her when she was trying to fight me. I don't even know how bad I wanted to go over there and fight her!

And that female that didn't like me, she just disappeared, I haven't seen her since that incident.

So the reason I am telling you all of this is because it had a big impact on my life. I went from a good, fun, and interesting life out in Federal Way to a not so great life in Seattle. If we hadn't moved I never would have had to face my summer of betrayal.

"Happy, smart, outrageous, and outgoing" — these are all words that thirteen-year-old **Jonishia Price** uses to describe herself. Jonishia is inspired by her family, though she loves talking on the phone and leaving the house. Her goals include finishing school, getting a good job, and one day having a family.

I WAS LUCKY THEY LET
ME GO TO THAT SCHOOL.
I WANTED TO PROVE TO
THEM I WASN'T LIKE MY
BROTHER.

A Very Different School
Shane McClellan

It was in sixth period when Viet, the security guard at Madison, pulled me out of class and brought me to the office. Someone said they saw me selling weed to some other guy after school. When they said they were going to search me, I thought I'd thrown anything bad out of my pockets the day before. Wrong. Soon it was official: I was suspended for possession of marijuana.

John Marshall Alternative School is very different from my old school, in a good way! At my old school, everyone was preppy with polo shirts and rich suburban parents, and no one was down for anything. All the teachers and staff were way uptight. I once almost got suspended for scaring a kid by saying, "Boo!" But at Marshall, they don't have a community of suburban kids with high standards.

And people here are not afraid to do stuff kids from my old school wouldn't.

I have to take two buses to get from Delridge to Greenlake, which is on the other side of Seattle. You would think I would have to wake up a lot earlier, but school here starts at 9:00 a.m., different from my old school's starting time of 7:45 a.m.

I thought I would miss my old friends, but not really. Just one of my homies, Ricky Santee. Another thing I hated about my old school were the teachers. All the teachers hated me. And I don't mean how those whiny kids say their teachers hate them. I mean those teachers hated me. Some of them would even acknowledge the fact that they hated me.

Teachers didn't trust me from the day I started at that school. My older brother used to go there, but he got in so much trouble he landed the school on the news! I was lucky they let me go to that school. I wanted to prove to them I wasn't like my brother, but that didn't work out very well.

I conclude that changing to this school has definitely changed my life and the future ahead of me. Besides the loss of a good friend, I think this change was one of my favorites.

You can often find thirteen-year-old **Shane McClellan** playing basketball or football. Music inspires him, as do his parents, and he plans on going to college after high school. What does he like most about himself? "Everything."

LET ME TELL YOU
SOMETHING: YOU
CHANGE ON THE
OUTSIDE, BUT ON THE
INSIDE YOU'RE WAY
DIFFERENT.

Many Years
Steven Nguyen

I was born in Seattle but raised in North Philly. Philly was a great place to live. Why? I had lots of relatives and lots of friends, but there was a lot of commotion going on at the same time, like gang fights and people cursing. Every morning you woke up and something would happen: a store would be robbed, people would get beat up for gang banging.

I lived in Philly for four years, then we drove from Philly to Seattle. It took us five days. We moved here because we wanted to see more of our family and relatives. This was my first time going back to Seattle since I was two or three years old. In Seattle we had no place to live, so we spent lots of nights at our cousin's house. Finally we had a house to live in and we stayed there for about a year until we moved to Beacon Hill. I realized that Beacon Hill had gang members, but they don't really go around and start beating up people. Gang members don't have to be really bad; they can sometimes be good people too.

When we moved to our new house in Seattle our family started to make more and more friends. In those years I changed quite a bit and grew a lot—about five to six inches.

My grades changed. I stopped getting lots of Cs and got lots of Bs and As. My attitude changed. Back then I got into lots of fights, but now I've stopped getting into fights a lot because Seattle seems like a good place not to fight. Also Seattle is a great place to live. I get to see the Space Needle and lots more.

When I grew up in Philly I wasn't too shy because I lived there for a while, but when I moved up to Seattle I became more and more shy. The first time I went to school here I was nervous, scared, and terrified. When I moved to my new house on Beacon Hill I didn't make friends. The first friend I made there was Chris. He came over and asked my brother and me to go shoot some hoops. I started to make more friends, then found even more at school.

Seattle schools felt so different from Philly. When you go to school in Philly lots and lots of people make fun of you every single day, but in Seattle schools it's different because here lots of kids don't talk back to their teachers. But in one way it's the same: the teacher is always bugging you to do your homework and stay awake in class. And if you don't go to school on time they will call home and bug you, saying your kid is not at school today.

One month into the new school year in seventh grade, something happened. I got called to the office for something that I didn't do—for arranging a fight. They said, "Steven, you are suspended for one whole semester." I got so mad for that.

Now my whole school year I have had to make new friends at John Marshall, too many to mention.

Now let me tell you all about what made me a different person. The change I went though was being raised in Philly and moving to Seattle and meeting new people, including some bad people. It is not a bad thing or a good thing to be different, that's just how it is.

When I was young I didn't dress in all these nice-looking clothes like South Pole, North Face, and Sean Jean. I didn't dress like a little kid. I dressed more like I came from the hood, but not like a thug that came from the hood. When you're little your parents teach you manners and being polite, but now I just act like that sometimes. Most of my changes are good changes because I've learned more stuff than when I was a little boy, and as I grow older I learn even more.

Let me tell you something: You change on the outside, but on the inside you're way different. From my point of view, on the outside I changed a lot. On the inside I changed too, but not as much as on the outside.

Fourteen-year-old **Steven Nguyen** is
happy that his writing is in a book, and
he had fun working on his story. His
main hobby is playing football, and he
plans to be a professional football player
one day. When pressed to describe himself, he says he's "fun to be with."

MY LITTLE SISTER WAS
SO MAD THAT DAY
BECAUSE THE COPS SAID
HE WAS COMING BACK
THE NEXT DAY. SHE
SOON FOUND OUT THAT
HE WASN'T COMING BACK;
SHE HATED HIM SO MUCH
FOR THAT REASON.

He Should Have Told Us
Monica Vargas

My life in Texas was not like other people's lives. Even when I was not at home it was not fun. I hated going to what I had to call "home" because of all the fighting there. My dad, Ernest, has dark brown hair and is really skinny. He looked like a ghost he was so pale. I started to notice a difference in his behavior when he started dating Janice. At night when I would go to bed and when I woke up in the morning, my little sister, Gabby, would be next to me. In the morning, I would turn around, kiss her on the forehead, and wake her up. The only reason she slept with me was because by the time we actually went to bed there would be glasses breaking and doors slamming. She was so terrified at night. This kind of stuff happened even when our friends came over, so I hated when people asked if they could come over. I was embarrassed.

We could only live day by day. This was my day, start to finish: I would wake up, kiss my little sister, and then wake her up. When we woke up, Jan was up and making us breakfast. We would get dressed and do our hair. Then we'd eat our breakfast and give Jan a hug and kiss. Before we left for the bus stop we would go in our dad's room and give him a hug and kiss. When all that was done, we'd ask Jan for our lunch money and then go to the bus stop.

I loved my school. I got to hang out with all my really good friends that I had known for two or three years. I mostly hung out with Tiffany and Keith. I loved all my teachers and going to school was nice because I got to get away from my house. I loved being at my house, just not when they were fighting. When I would get on the bus to go home I would usually get in a fight with the only girl in the school I did not like. I cannot say hate because I do not hate anyone. Hate is a really strong word.

On Fridays I would usually go to Tiffany's house. Tiffany is fourteen years old with beautiful brown hair and eyes. She always put herself down and said she was really ugly but she was not. So on Friday I rode the bus home with Tiffany and Keith. When we got off the bus, we went to Tiffany's house. Tiffany and I always had fun and we could connect with each other. Friday nights I would go to Keith's because on Saturdays and Sundays Tiffany went to her dad's. I would stay with Keith until Sunday night. He lived with his dad and stepmom, two little sisters, and one little brother. Their house and Tiffany's house were my homes away from home. I always had fun at Keith's house no matter how much his dad made fun of me. One time I knew he cared because he told me if I ever needed a place to go, I could go to their house. Then on Sunday nights, I either had my daddy come and pick me up or Keith's stepmom would drive me home.

Then Jan and my dad decided they could not get along anymore. Right away my dad had a new girlfriend, Cathy. She could be really nice at times. Just like Jan, there was a lot of fighting, but it was even worse. For some reason my dad really loved her. They were together a lot longer than he and Jan were. And they are still in love today. The only reason they fought so much was the drugs. Not just any drugs but methamphetamines, which I think are the worst of all of them. My dad was always either stoned or asleep. That sums up his life when he was doing drugs. I hated him for that reason. I knew he was doing it but I wanted him to be honest with me and tell me himself.

January 8, 2007 is the day my dad got arrested for possession of methamphetamines. He had decided to go and show off his truck to his friend and someone called the cops because they were suspicious. When my dad saw the cops he had drugs on him so he panicked. Instead of being normal and coming in through the driveway, he came in the back way. This is why they got so suspicious, so they searched his truck and found methamphetamines, and what was on him got him up to twenty-five years in prison.

My little sister was so mad that day because the cops said he was coming back the next day. She soon found out that he wasn't coming back; she hated him so much for that reason. I think she doesn't really hate him, but instead she's angry with him because he did not tell her the truth. She was only ten at the time. She just wanted him to tell her, instead of the cops. As much as he tried, he could not.

We made plans to go see him the following Saturday. That did not happen and was not going to. Three days later my mom, Laura, was in Texas, ready to take us back with her to Seattle. My mom is thirty-five-years old with blonde hair that is almost always crimped because she got it curled tons of times. When she picked us up from school there was only one person I really wanted to say goodbye to and that was Tiffany. Of course I cried. When we arrived in Washington we had to stay with my auntie Sarah because we did not have a home.

Now I have decided that I loved my home in Texas and I wish every day I was back there. I want my dad to get his life back together so he can raise us the way he was supposed to. At the same time, I love being here in Seattle and spending the quality time with my mom that I never got because of my dad. I love all my new friends, Saffia, Amira, Daquan, and everyone else. These people have made me feel very welcome and I am ready to love and start new relationships.

Dad, I am going to see you as soon as possible and I love you a lot, a lot. But you really need to get your life together.

Fourteen-year-old **Monica Vargas**
thinks that this book project is great. "I
love to write," she says. She also enjoys
hanging out with friends, and her big
sister, Stephanie Kay, is her inspiration.
Her goals are to graduate from college
and become a published writer – again.

...ALL I ASK IS THAT
YOU PLEASE REMEMBER
THROUGH OUR DIVINE
DIVIDE THAT I AM STILL
YOUR BLOOD, I AM STILL
YOUR SKIN...

Bone Dust
Amber DeLorme

Dear cold wind bitter breath lost passion standing five feet five inches
    too short in torn denim and soft skin,
I forgive you.
As I sit here folding inwards,
pen held lightly,
And bones numbing softly,
I forgive you.
And though you often blame me for our cold nights, bruised fists,
    and drug addictions in order to keep your own head above ground,
I forgive you.
This is transition.

See,
I have been asked many times where I come from,
And always, I reply with "See" not "Sea,"
As in the city I grew up in
or "Sea," the water that gave it life,
But "SEE." As in See Me.
See the scars on my skin and the white of my wrists,
I came from bone.
My life was a rescue story.
She saved herself—for me.
But still from the moment of my conception I was never content with
    simplicity,
and through a miracle of rebellion I clawed my way from my mother's
    womb to rest gently in her rib cage,
milk white, blood prints, bone child.
And I fed off her marrow as she lived off my life, we were ocean
    tide...
Sand breathing softly,
Ocean reaching slowly,
and entangled so gently as to be nearly one and the same.

But things didn't stay that way,
And I've grown stunted from the little pieces of her still inside me,
Bone fragments and milk dreams
Some from birth, some from life,

See I was a happy kid,
Don't get me wrong.
I didn't understand as a child that recycled excuses & substance
    misusage weren't acceptable codes of conduct for single broke down
    parents.
In fact I didn't even understand our own definition of broke down
    when she
Laid down after a night of exposing her tits for horny forty-some
    things who hid their dark circle guilt eyes behind the twenties she
    danced for.

I kept things simple.
Like how that time I went to the beach & saw an elephant
Defiantly overpowered the memory of
Age three
My father holding my mother down
with her blood blossoming knuckles staining the bed as I watched
  through broken breath
fighting against the sharp pain bursting across my own face.
See, I barely even remember being hit.
I don't think I wanted to, because when you're a child
family's all you have.
I was just trying to make mine work.
But somewhere around the age of thirteen I began to realize that this
  was NOT
how things should have been.
And they didn't have to be.
So I started punching back.

But now I'm
Snipping softly at my flesh as I try to find where we separate once
  more.
Because I'm breathing but not living.
I'm reaching for her threads trying to unravel,
NEEDING to unravel
our stitching.
See,
I have all the answers but no way to untangle them from her or my
  self – I
Smell her vodka breath and cold fists on bus rides sometimes and peel
  away at the corners like I did the school textbooks of my youth,
only then, I didn't understand that there were no answers to the
  equations describing the influence of her foggy eyes, and the bruises
  we christened on each other.
It was something like initial impact (my head in her hands smashed a
  against bathroom mirrors) times March 24th (the day her rescue
  story fell short with a hopeful handful of valiums and wine stained

lips) divided by the time it took me to feel more than just wind
  beneath my feet again (the day I picked up the pen for the first time
  and found break beats hiding underneath my pillow).
And only then I didn't understand that there were no excuses for the
  embarrassment I felt as a child when asked by my fifth grade
  teacher to write an essay on my first memory...
Her bent over a coke tray,
My hands reaching in frustration,
I wanted to try so badly.
And eventually I did.
I was – Reaching and
tumbling
Limbs askew,
Cutting
Ripping
Ripping her, and me,
Blood,
Blood and bone dust
Back arched
Sweat—sliding down my ribs...
But I awoke, eventually.
And I found myself in the shadows between these starch white pages.
And you weren't there.

So this is me
Reclaiming those broken threads just long enough to maybe empty
  your lungs of that stale air and wash over your skin once more...
So—let me once more hang my hands above your heart and play
  softly the beat of my pulse along your ribcage,
Milk white bone-bearer,
To maybe help bring clarity upon your own life.
And all I ask is that you please remember through our divine divide
  that I am still your blood, I am still your skin,
And when dawn rises upon your deteriorating faith in once night life
  contained in empty liquor bottles,
Remember,

That I am the only one who holds the scars of your womb and knows
  your genetic code by heart,
MY heart.
And remember,
That as dawn rises I will be the only one to forgive your nature and
  love your soiled skin.

I forgive you.

What word best describes **Amber
DeLorme**? "'Aesthetics,' in bold
letters," says the seventeen-year-old.
You can often find Amber performing
slam and spoken word, making music,
admiring flicks, and "midnight
adventuring." She says she's inspired
by the Youth Speaks crew.

MY LIFE HAS BEEN
FROM HELL AND BACK.
I'VE HAD A HARD PAST
AND DONE A LOT OF
MOVING.

From Hell And Back
D'Andre Glaspy

My life has been from hell and back. I've had a hard past and done a lot of moving around, living in garages, basements, and cars. Lots of people think their lives suck because they have to share their room with a sibling. I would have loved that. I would have loved a room.

My mom and I had a slumlord who wouldn't fix anything. He kicked us out of our apartment. I was jumping from place to place for a while. I mean, I didn't have a pot to piss in. This is when I moved in with my uncle.

For two years, my uncle mistreated me.

The first month I was there, he told me my mom didn't love me. He told me I wasn't going to be anything. He even waved his gun at me, made me do his laundry, iron his clothes—everything that he was supposed to do, I did. He was the epitome of pain. After everything was done, I couldn't even watch television because I had to hear his mouth about having an 87.9% B+.

Then he sort of cooled off, but not really. One time he told me I could come in an hour after dark. I was across the street in clear sight. It was summer and it didn't get dark until around 8:00 p.m., so I came in at nine. When he got home at ten, his girlfriend told him what time I came in. He was furious and he took it out on me. I looked pretty bad the next day. All my friends at school saw my face and asked me what happened. I told them and they told me I should tell someone, but I didn't, like an idiot.

The next time he hit me, I told my mom. It was hard to convince her at first.

"The next time he tells you I did something wrong, you should some over and investigate," I told her. "Come and see my wounds."

So she did. One day she popped up unannounced. She said she would come and get me the next night. When she left, he made me scrub every inch of his house, top to bottom.

The next day my mom came in her truck and she and my uncle got into a fight. My mom helped me pack my things and we left. We went to her boyfriend's house and that's where I live now. It is a much better environment for me. I only need one more thing and that is a house for me and my family. I don't know if I'll get my own house, but we'll figure something out. Hey, at least I'm almost out of hell.

"Strong-hearted," "large-minded," "kind," and "stern"—these are some of the words thirteen-year-old **D'Andre Glaspy** uses to describe himself. His mother, sister, grandma, and the rapper Tupac Shakur inspire D'Andre, and he would like to become a mathematician or scientist. He feels the story he wrote for this book was a "good way to express my past and move on to the future."

WHEN MY STEPDAD WAS
KILLED, I HAD TO GO
THROUGH A TRANSFOR-
MATION IN THE WAY I
THOUGHT ABOUT LIFE.

You Don't Know Anything About What I Know
Gabrielle Moore

The definition of change is to undergo transformation, transition, or substitution. In some twisted sense that is exactly what I went through ... all of them. When my stepdad was killed, I had to go through a transformation in the way I thought about life. I had to go through a transition in terms of the freedom and material items I was accustomed to having. And I had to go through a substitution of a guy who was my dad and who I didn't care for, and a woman who made me call her mom who wasn't really my mom.

In this story I will refer to my stepdad as my dad or father and I will to my real father as my biological father. So that means when I say parents I mean my stepdad and my mother. As you'll see, my mom and stepdad were no saints. Although I don't place blame on one or the other, this is how I see things.

One of my first experiences of change occurred when I was only nine years old. I had already seen way too much for my age, and my life was becoming more and more complicated. Rather than playing with my brother and the rest of the kids like I used to, I was noticing more of my parents fighting and arguing. I was staying real close to home because my heart was going to crack into tiny microscopic pieces if my parents were to separate. They did almost everything they possibly could do to make it work for my siblings and me, but they were getting tired. The thunder was only building up and everybody could feel it. About three months before my dad was killed, slowly but surely the fighting became more frequent. The thunder finally arose and its disturbing presence was not welcome, but it flowed and tore everything up in its path anyway.

The last straw was drawn when my mom found out that my dad had a daughter the same age as my youngest sister, Timmi, who was two at the time. My mom was hurt immensely; she really loved my dad and although he loved her too, there was no way to take back the pain he had exposed her to.

My mom found out about this little fleshy skeleton in my dad's closet one day as she went through her regular morning routine. That day, she walked into our room feeling good, and then she saw a little girl no older that a year and a half with a gap in between her teeth (a trait that all of my dad's children have) and she just starting going crazy and acting really weird. What my dad did caused a great deal of pain in her and she went crazy… literally.

My mom kicked my dad out, ordered us not to open the door for him, and got the locks changed. One time, when she was at work, my dad came home. We had disobeyed her orders and let him in. We felt that we couldn't just pick one parent or the other, and I let my brother talk me into opening the door. She abruptly came home early. My dad had to climb out of the bathroom window so she wouldn't catch him. But she knew that he was there because she had seen his car parked two blocks away, and she was yelling and screaming because she didn't want us to let him in and we did it anyway.

After that she took all of his clothes out and put them on the front

BURNING THE PAST

porch and poured bleach all over them. My brother and I were crying hysterically because we thought he was never going to come back. My dad was the only fatherly figure I had. My biological father wasn't in my life, and my mom treated me slightly different than she did my brother. My dad stepped up and always did for me like no other.

My mom took every single picture she had of him and her and cut his face out of them, then threw them away. My brother and I told her that we were going to my auntie's house, but instead we went to the dumpster and took all the pictures that she had thrown away and hid them outside. When she left we patched up all the pictures and put them back outside so that she wouldn't see them. But then one day it started to rain and my brother ran outside and got the pictures. They were slightly wet but you could still see the faces and we hid them in our auntie Big Momma's room.

One day, on the sneak, my dad came to the house and saw all the stuff from his closet outside with bleach all over it. He broke down, and that was the first time I had ever seen him cry and I cried right along with him. It broke my young heart to see my daddy cry, so I was right there with him until he stopped and gave my brother and me some money to go to the store to get some candy and food. Although we didn't want to leave him, we didn't want to lose him either. We obeyed him and went to the store. Although we tried, it was so hard to forget what we had just seen.

Not long after that, my mom disappeared.

When she came back to her senses she returned to Seattle. One day Auntie Janell took my siblings and me to the family fun center. My mom had told us to meet her there. We were playing and having a ball when my mom called Auntie Janell and told her that she was outside. When we went out to meet her, she was crying and my brother and I were asking her what was wrong with her. What it was was that she didn't know how to explain to her children that she was going to go to jail for a long time. All the while she was holding my beautiful baby sister. She gave us each some money and gave the remaining balance to Auntie Janell. About five minutes later a cop car came and they arrested her. I was crushed to little bite-size pieces because I knew what was going on.

313

My mom had just turned herself in so that she would be able to do right by her children; she didn't want to live life on the run. In my years of growing up I was never mad at her but I was hurt because I thought she left me. I will always will respect my mom for being a dignified woman and doing that. Her plan was to turn herself in and request bail and, with a good lawyer, she would only have to serve 90 days and a little while on home detention. It didn't happen as she planned, though, and she ended up serving three years in Western State Mental Hospital.

My dad, being a good guy, was going to bail her out of jail, but they had denied her bail. So he took my brother, my baby sister, and me to my grandma Norma's house, and we stayed there for a couple of days. We had fun but I knew there was more to the story than just going to spend time with our other grandmother (what can I say, I was a very skeptical child), so I kept my ears open. One day I heard my dad telling my grandma Norma that he wanted to take us to California. I think this was a week or two before he died. Grandma Norma told him not to take me away from my biological father without getting his permission first. So my siblings and I spent some more time with my grandma while he got things situated with my mom first.

Later that month my dad was shot five times in the heart and killed in front of the Columbia Center plaza. I have always thought that only if I had been his real child and he hadn't had to get permission from my biological father to take us to California, he wouldn't have been killed.

A day or so before he died my siblings and I went to spend some time with my biological father. So I was at my his house when my family told me my dad had been killed. I was so heartbroken, I cried for hours. Nobody could console me. While my family hovered around the table and told me what happened, the glass tabletop slowly filled with water from my tears. How could it be my dad had just been shot and my mother could be no comfort to me either because she was in jail? My dad was the only person I had ever loved that much other than my mom. Even though I wasn't his child, he never treated me differently. He bought me stuff when he bought my brother stuff, he told everybody that I was his daughter, and that's how all of his homies and family treated me. When he passed away his homies would give me money and treat me the same as they did my little brother Terrell and my little sister Timmi, his real children.

I think I took it the hardest because I was the oldest and I understood about death, and he was also my strongest source of love. My siblings and I got separated. I had to stay in Washington with my biological father, who all of a sudden wanted to play mighty father and wouldn't let me go to California with my brother and sister. That tore me up even more. My brother was like my son, we were like twins, we fought together, stole together, did everything you could think of together. He was my ace. When my brother and sister went to California, they took half of my heart with them. I was all alone in this world.

As a result, I was awful; I just didn't care anymore. I had lost my mom to the system, my brother and sister to California, and my dad through the life of the gangster in love. At the time, I was going to a school called Daniel T. Elementary. It was seriously difficult to cope with the children that kept asking me what happened and if I was okay, and to talk to them if I needed any help. What the hell? They are little kids just like me. They don't know anything about what I know.

My biological father had a girlfriend that I absolutely despised. I went to so many schools and didn't get to grow up like a regular girl. I was treated with the best love that he knew how to provide, which wasn't much. When I first moved in with him, he lived right next to the Speedy Mart on a four way stop going in to Renton and Skyway, in a little brown duplex. Although I loathed the situation, I was never really lonely. I had two stepbrothers and another on the way. I had magnificent times at school. I loved school because I hated the idea of coming home.

When we moved away from that house, we moved to the South End on Alaska Street. On the morning of my first birthday after my dad's passing, I cried so hard because I had never had a birthday without him or my mom before. My biological father heard me and he came in to my room, the one I shared with my little sister Adonaca. He asked me why I was crying and I told him, "I miss my dad." I didn't mean to hurt his feelings but I did. He was crushed. He called me a punk and told me to stop crying; he told me that my stepdad wouldn't want me to cry.

I just didn't want to be there, I missed my dad, plus I wasn't used to getting off-brand clothing and a low quantity of it at that. I was spoiled—what could I say? Then came the sixth grade. I was extremely bad. I was rarely on time to class and I never did my work. I became worse when my mom got out of jail. I was feeling my oats. Summer was around the corner and I was getting ruthless. Then I found out that I had failed all of my classes, so I had to go to summer school. My biological father was furious. I had never seen him so angry before, and I kind of enjoyed it.

Summer school started and I was pissed because I was mad at my biological father for making me go, and my stepmom for even being alive. So on the first day I was really bad. I knew I was going to be in trouble. The teacher was going to kick me out of summer school, but fortunately she allowed me to come back to her class.

Around this time, my mom took me to a family gathering, and at the time I didn't know that one of my aunties had told my mom that I had got in a lot of trouble and my stepmom was talking crazy to me. My mom wasn't mad about my biological father whooping me; she just didn't want my stepmom putting her hands on me. On the day of the family picnic my mom told my family that she knew I had gotten into trouble. My mom was like a volcano steaming; she hadn't caused an eruption yet but you could see one was clearly near. My mom, my cousin Trina, and I walked into my biological father's house. I went to my room and put down my purse, and I took my shoes off. I heard arguing; my mom was about to beat up my stepmom over what they were going to do for my birthday tomorrow. I started screaming and trying to go to my mom, but my stepmom was pulling me back and I swung, connected, and ran outside. Then I ran all the way up the hill to Genesee Street. My mom was calling for me to come but I wouldn't because my biological father was going to take me. I was barefooted, running, screaming, and crying all at the same time.

Later that day my mother dropped me off at my cousin's house, where my auntie Big Momma was. My mom didn't stay but she told me that she would be back to get me later. But she didn't come until the afternoon of the next day. Happy Birthday, Gabby. It's my birthday and my mom isn't here to greet me. Wow, what a twelfth birthday. She finally came and told me that I was going to be staying with my Granny Pooh. On that day I thought my prayers had been answered. I was blessed to have a new beginning. But will it last? To be continued…

Sixteen-year-old **Gabrielle Moore**
would like everyone to hear her untold
story. Her goals are to graduate from
high school with a grade point average
of 3.5 or higher and then go on to college. Her mother, God, and her grandmother inspire her. What does Gabby
like most about herself? "My ability to
adapt to different situations."

MY PARENTS DIDN'T AND
STILL DON'T LISTEN TO
THE SAME MUSIC AS
EACH OTHER. I ALWAYS
THOUGHT THAT MY DAD
AND MOM WOULD LISTEN
TO THE SAME MUSIC.

Life is Full of Surprises
Avery Austin

I have moved a lot my whole life. I started to understand why at about age ten. When I was born my mom and dad got a divorce and I didn't get to see my dad a lot. They got a divorce because my dad smoked and he didn't want to smoke around me. I had to stay with my mom on my grandma's property. I didn't like the fact that we were living there without paying rent. Back then I didn't know why I had to stay there but I understand now.

My mom and I moved out of my grandma's when I was about four years old. I was glad to leave because my mom and grandpa were fighting all the time. We moved to Anacortes because my mom's new boyfriend, Dave, works in the port as a longshoreman. Now they are married. Around this time is when I started to fight with other kids and hate the world in general. Why, you may ask? Because I felt hurt by others, and picked on. There was always so much fighting.

About a year later I moved in with my dad because my mom and Dave were fighting a lot. My dad lived in a small apartment in Shoreline. We had to stay with a good friend and split the rent. His name was Jay. Because he had two kids, Tie who was seven and Ein who was four, I had to share a room.

It was very hectic there because we fought a lot, even though my dad and Jay got along well. I personally have a lot of bad memories from that place, most of them having to do with beating people up. In some ways I was popular, but in some ways I wasn't. I had a few real friends but no girlfriend. Most girls did not like me because I was mean and I beat up the most popular girl's boyfriend.

At this time, if I could have had a choice I would have gone back to my grandparents' house. My grandma has two ATVs and one hundred acres of woods and fields. It was better than nothing and it would only be my cousin Tony and me. My cousin Tony lives there half the time but the other half he lives with his mom. He is one of my best friends. He is in alternative school and has had some trouble with the law.

If I were to go back to live with my grandma, grandpa, and great grandpa, this is how it would be. I would probably get everything I want and I would weigh eight hundred pounds because I eat nothing but sugar when I am there. I usually have cake and ice cream for breakfast. I am a sucker for angel food cake. But my dad and I stayed in Shoreline until we could afford our own house in Ballard.

Now a lot has changed. I have more rules and chores at Dad's, like doing the dishes and taking out the garbage. I wish I had fewer rules and I wish I could play more video games, but instead I skateboard a lot now. I have to go outside and I wish I could be inside more. The music I listen to has changed, too. I used to listen to nothing but rap, but now I listen to nothing but punk and Insane Clown Posse, which is ghetto rap. My parents didn't and still don't listen to the same music as each other. I always thought that my dad and mom would listen to the same music. They were married and they had to listen to something, but my mom listens to rap and my dad listens to punk.

If you made it to here you probably liked my story or you were forced to read it. If you were forced by your teacher or parents, I'm sorry. If you liked it, thanks and good reading.

Twelve-year-old **Avery Austin** likes his hair a lot and is inspired by ponies and his friend, Chris. What is one of his goals? "To become the best skater."

HOW COULD SOMETHING
SO CLOSED OFF
AND UGLY TURN SO
BEAUTIFUL SO QUICKLY?

Blood And Butterflies

Breanna Alexander

Sunday morning. Seeing the sun peek over the horizon in colors of pink, red, and blue. Another day just like every other day, pointless, boring, and tiring. I knew soon enough this day would end and another day of pointless worry and distress would begin. Nothing could excite my mood. Nothing ever did.

As I opened my window to taste the fresh, crisp air of spring, I saw an object the color of bark but no bigger than a mouse. A cocoon hanging on my windowsill, hard as a rock. I had never really seen a cocoon up close before, so this—for the first time in a long time—excited my mood. I tapped it gently, cold as the air that surrounded it but soft as cotton.

I smiled and left my room to shower and dress. I missed my dad; I didn't get to visit him that weekend. My parents divorced some time ago; I lived with my mom and got to visit my father on weekends. I guess I even missed my brother and sister, even though we weren't always close. They lived with our father.

I walked out to the living room to look for my mother; she was there, eating and watching TV, same old routine.

Later that night I visited my windowsill cocoon. I swear it had gotten brighter, possibly bigger as well, but I didn't think much of it.

That week at school was the usual hell as always. I didn't want that hell to come back, so I ditched. I felt free, almost alive. I wanted that ecstasy of freedom to come back to me, so I did it again. I ditched until it was the last month of school. By then I had gotten into a lot of trouble for my absences. I still didn't care: I felt free, alive! I finally did something that may not have been in my best interests, but I did it because I wanted to. I never wanted that feeling to go away. So I continued to do it until one day when my mother called the police on me. I still didn't care.

I attended school for a while, the freedom went away and the feeling of my ecstasy went with it. But time passed by and I soon regained my freedom. School was out. Still, I did the same routine every day at my mom's; it numbed my mind until I spaced the day away.

More time passed and I wanted to get away, not just for a weekend at my dad's, but forever. The best I could do without it being illegal was move into my dad's, so we talked about it and it was final. I was moving in. I was so happy I packed my things most precious and drove to Seattle. My mother was sad of course, but how could she be so selfish? Would she rather have me be depressed living with her than being happy at my dad's? I'd still be able to see her every weekend; she didn't need to smother me.

But again, I didn't care. I was content. The summer passed as my dad, Laura (dad's fiancée), my brother, my sister, and I moved into a bigger house so we all could get our own rooms.

I finally finished unpacking by September. Of course, I didn't forget my most precious thing of all: my windowsill cocoon. I taped it to the edge of my window, checking the temperature to make sure it was not too hot or cold.

My father had gotten me a packet that told all about this really good school he wanted me to go to. He thought it would be best for me, and I did too. I read the packet and fell in love with the school. They had an art program. I'd be able to express myself freely in the fine arts, my favorite subject. I love to sketch and paint; the flow of the colors combine together to make a beautiful work of art. I wanted to create beauty to share with the world. I was so excited to go to the Center School; sad to find out I had to wait on a list to go there.

A couple months passed, and I still didn't get enrolled into that school. It took longer than my father and I thought it would. So we went the alternative way, John Marshall Alternative School, to be exact.

At first it was nothing special, just another bum school, where delinquents and troublemakers go to right what they've done wrong. But soon enough I met people there who were so nice to me, though I didn't want to make any friends. I was fine on my own, or so I thought. They wouldn't leave me alone at first, always greeting me, wanting me to eat with them during lunch. I tried to act cold towards them but they stayed the same, always being nice to me. So I did what anyone would do in a situation such as that: I caved in.

I finally decided to eat lunch with them, and now I still do, and even regret not going with them before. They were so nice to me. It was warming the ice around my heart, and I returned the kindness. Soon enough, that wasn't the only thing I felt, because we had so much fun just hanging out together it made me more like the playful, kind person I had once been very long ago.

But not all the feelings were good. It's like all the emotions I missed out on regarding my family and friends, or just growing up, all hit me at once. I became depressed. Happy at school, but depressed at home. I felt as though the only thing I could do to get rid of the emotional pain was to make it physical, so I did. I'd hurt myself on purpose in order for my mind to focus on the physical pain so the emotional pain would stop, and it did. At the time, I thought that was the only way to make it go away. While my family lay asleep, I'd do terrible things to myself almost every night. And as I lay there, arms red and sticky with my own blood, I realized that it had to stop. I'd do anything to stop hurting myself, but then what could I do to stop the emotional pain?

I created my own little fantasy world, where I had friends, just like the ones at school who cared, only cyber. I developed a liking of teen chat rooms. I met new people there who lived all over the world and some of them became really close friends. That was my new routine: school, home, computer, eat, sleep. Repeat.

I wanted to feel happy 24/7, so I'd make myself happy. Role-playing fantasy adventure games in a whole new world where vampires, demons, faeries, angels, and many other mythical creatures were born. I'd go on quests, defeat evil monsters, and save a magical realm. My fantasy world was exciting, it was fun, and it made me happy.

Then one day I woke up and was oddly depressed. Yes, I was mostly always depressed when not with my friends or role-playing, but that day was different. Normally I'd be excited to see my friends in the morning, but that day, all I could think about was how worthless I felt. Even looking at my windowsill cocoon made me depressed. I went to school without any excitement or even the desire to see my friends, and that made it worse. They tried making me happy by paying attention to me more than normal, asking me what was wrong, and telling me that they were there for me. But it didn't help. I just felt more and more worthless and depressed than ever before.

At lunch, it was the same thing, everyone eating together and hanging out, nothing special, but I just couldn't take it anymore. I'd held my feelings in for too long and it was so painful and it hurt even more that nobody noticed when I was really depressed.

I burst out crying and I couldn't stop; all the tears were just flowing out all at once and it felt good. But a strange thing happened. Everyone rushed to my side to cradle and comfort me. I wasn't used to this, all this love; I was used to crying in my room alone at night.

All of a sudden I felt loved, not worthless. I felt warm, even happy. I loved these people, my friends. They made all the negative feelings I had that day go away and for the rest of the day I was laughing and enjoying myself, as I should. I felt so happy and loved my friends a hundred times more.

I went home that day to check on my cocoon, but it was gone. I looked around frantically to see if it fell. There it lay, the remains of it on the floor, as if someone ripped it to shreds. I was so sad; the tears welled in my eyes. Then all of a sudden I saw something orange and black out of the corner of my eye. The creature in the cocoon had hatched out of its dark prison and survived to see the beautiful, colorful world around it. It was now a beautiful butterfly.

How could something so closed off and ugly turn so beautiful so quickly? I caught the butterfly in my bare hands and ran down stairs, slamming the door open. I walked outside in the humid air of spring, opened my palms and there sat the butterfly and all the bliss it had to offer the world. It flew out of my hand with grace. I watched it until it flew right out of sight. I sat on the grass, full of serenity. I felt calm, I felt loved, I felt happy.

I still have those feelings. Every now and then I have my off days, but I am so grateful I made the decision to move in with my dad, to go to school at John Marshall, and to start eating lunch with them, my friends. So that's it, case closed.

If you see fifteen-year-old **Breanna Alexander** wearing a pair of head-phones, chances are she's gaining inspiration from music. She describes herself as random, spontaneous, funny, and a sweetheart who's very protective of her friends. One of her goals is to do better in school. Outside the classroom, you can find her making art, taking photos, writing, and singing.

ACKNOWLEDGMENTS

The Students Who Wrote These Pieces

Breanna Alexander
Avery Austin
Daquan Bowens
Adrian Bram
Rasheeda Davis
Akeisha Deloach
Amber DeLorme
Paolo Del Donno
DeAndre Eaton
Amira Elhuraibi
Saffia Elhuraibi
Sthefano Esteves
D'Andre Glaspy
Kathy Graves
Ashley Mackay
Courtney Hill

Douglas Ho
Heather Hoyt
Jessica Hoyt
Tallon Johnson
Trevor Jones
Shauna Lee
Christina Leslie
Emma Lopez
Steven McAlpin
Shane McClellan
Schyler Mishra
Hana Mohamed
Gabrielle Moore
Carissa Muller
Christina Nguyen
Steven Nguyen

Devonte Parson
Jonishia Price
Vanessa Quiroz
Jami Ram
Collin Richter
David Ryan Richter
Asuzena Rodriguez
Deondre Simons
Unique Smith
Veronica Tinajero
C.J. Thomas
Anthony D. Vaughn
Lemara Vaiese
Monica Vargas
Amanda Williams

John Marshall Teachers and Other Important Staff Who Helped Make This Book Happen

Jeff Calderwood
Sheila de la Cruz
Audra Gallegos
John Hannay
Susan Knutsen
Jean Littlefield

Gordon MacDougall
Jeanne Schmidt
Dennis Sipos
Jibril Rashid
Carol Wakefield

The People Who Lost the Most Sleep Over This Project

Jim Beckmann, Audra Gallegos, Jennie Shortridge, Bill Thorness

The Buck Stops Here Person

Teri Hein

The 826 Seattle Tutors

Andrea Baer
Jim Beckmann
Janet Buttenwieser
April Christiansen
Martin Cron
Elisa Ding
Bronwyn Doyle
Jennifer Borges Foster
Tim Gadbois

Alison Galinsky
Michael Gilbert
Izabelle Gorczynski
Cary Ann Greif
Marc Greilsamer
Pam Heath
Teri Hein
Emily Irwin
Nancy Johnson

Terrilyn Johnson
LeAnne Laux-Bachand
Marc Moquin
Jessica Murphy
Jennie Shortridge
Bill Thorness
Mike Ullmann
Julia Warth

Graphic Design and Production
Julia Littlefield

Audio Recording
Praxia Apostle

Copyediting

Kathy Bremner
Bronwyn Doyle
Angela J. Fountas
LeAnne Laux-Bachand
Rose Pike

Ann Senechal
Jennie Shortridge
Bill Thorness
Mike Ullmann

Author Photographs
Carla Leonardi

Author Biographies
LeAnne Laux-Bachand

PTA For A Day Presidents and General Publishing Party Organizers
Nancy Johnson, Ellen Sisk

We gratefully acknowledge the people and
organizations who funded this project

Barrie Trinkle, Washington State Arts Commision,
and The Starbucks Foundation

ABOUT 826 SEATTLE

826 Seattle is a nonprofit organization dedicated to supporting students ages 6-18 with their creative and expository writing skills, and to helping teachers inspire their students to write. Our services are structured around our belief that great leaps in learning can happen with one-on-one attention and that strong writing skills are fundamental to future success. With this in mind we provide drop-in tutoring, field trips, after school workshops, in-school tutoring, help for English language learners, and assistance with student publications. All of our free programs are challenging and enjoyable, and ultimately strengthen each student's power to express ideas effectively, creatively, confidently, and in his or her individual voice.

All donations to 826 Seattle are tax deductible. For more information please visit our website: www.826seattle.org.

826
SEATTLE

CD TRACK LIST

BURNING THE PAST
ESSAY EXERPTS READ BY THE AUTHORS

1	Intro: Audra Gallegos
2	Opening
3	C.J. Thomas
4	Akeisha Deloach
5	Sthefano Esteves
6	Amber DeLorme
7	Paolo Del Donno
8	Tallon Johnson
9	David Ryan Richter
10	Hana Mohamed
11	Rasheeda Davis
12	Monica Vargas
13	Adrian Bram
14	Stephen McAlpin
15	Closing